I0427640

A Manifesto For
The Common Man

by:

DARIUS **R**ADMANESH

First Paper Back,June 2011
ISBN-13: 9781500407186
ISBN-10: 1500407186
Cover Design: Darius Radmanesh
Interior Design: Darius Radmanesh

Readers may contact the author at: Darius.Radmanesh@gmail.com
Published by CreateSpace, a DBA of On-Demand Publishing, LLC.

DEDICATION

This publication **IS DEDICATED** to the noble cause of the common man.

**High poverty level and homelessness
the byproduct of Corporate Capitalism.**

Homeless people go unseen everyday, as passersby ignore their existence on sidewalks, in parks, in subway stations. People have these attitudes that they're lazy, that they deserve what they get, they haven't worked hard, they're just looking for a handout. and people with these attitudes lack compassion,. People who live in countries like the United States and the United Kingdom that have more capitalistic economies and offer fewer social services, are more likely to believe personal failings are the primary cause of homelessness and feel less compassion for homeless people. Meanwhile, these countries have higher rates of homelessness than, for example, Germany, where there is a guaranteed minimum income, more generous UNEMPLOYMENT benefits and more rigorous tenants rights. "

" What kind of world do we live in today I ask?, where ones worth and value is judged and determined not by the principles and virtues of integrity, honesty, loyalty, morality and honor. But rather by the jinglings of coins and wads of notes one carries in his or her pocket?. These are the only recognisable virtues and Worth's of man, in this empty, dark and gilded shell which we so shamefully fancy, to be a civilised world!."

- Darius Radmanesh

In a country well governed, poverty is something to be ashamed of. In a country badly governed, wealth is something to be ashamed of.

-Confucius

Having been poor is no shame, but being ashamed of it, is.

-Benjamin Franklin

A PERSONAL NOTE

This publication is not edited nor is it polished, because the purpose behind its publication was not with the intention of wining a Pulitzer Prize. But rather it is intended to educate, enlighten and inspire, and to be read only by those whom judge a book by its content and substance and not by its cover. If you are one of those whom places more emphases on the exterior rather then inner worth, then this book is not for you.

-Darius Radmanesh

CHAPTER

ONE

I think that it is absolutely imperative that I make one point abandontly clear as to what was the source or inspiration for my 'stance on severing all contacts and affiliations between the wealthy Corporate elite, from the state. My views stem largely from my observing and studying history, and learning from the mistakes made by previous civilizations. Civilizations for example such as ancient Greece and even more importantly ancient Rome, mainly the Roman Republican era.

It is in this era which I strongly believe we may find a solution to many of the issues and crises which our society is facing today. For It was during this time, there was a strict law put in to effect by the Roman Senate, at the early stage of the Roman Republic, which prohibited all members of the wealthy (Equestrian) merchant class the corporates of that time from taking any direct or indirect roll in the political affairs of the state. This included their inability to run for public office or to make any kind of financial contributions to a candidates campaign running for public office.

In addition all Roman senators weir also in turn prohibited from becoming either directly or indirectly involved in the Commercial sector as well, which meant that they weir not permitted by law to either invest or to hold any kind of financial interests in any of the businesses or industries at the time. The reasoning for this was very simple, this was because from a very early stage.

The Romans, had learned a great deal about how politics can be manipulated, subverted and corrupted by the wealthy merchant elite, so to curve legislation to serve there own business interests. Which they weir also fully aware would not always necessarily be in the overall best interest of not only the Roman citizens but also the state as well. As we can see in history, so long as the Romans adhered to this law and principle. There society grew and flourished.

However as time progressed and the worlds wealth began to poor in to the city state....More and more people became infected with the fever for the comforts and many luxuries which the City had now been filed with transformed the Romans themselves.

Thus the in fluxed of such extremes of wealth and poverty that sharpened social and economic conflict within the Roman state, dramatically changed the countryside as small farms gave way to large plantations, and luxurious villas. Consequently many farmers lost their homes, lands and farms and migrated to Rome and other cities. Immense wealth inflamed the ambitions of Roman nobles who struggled for personal domination and the hording of wealth rather then upholding the interests and well being of the Roman people and collective rule.

More and More senators began ignoring this law and at first began dabbling in to private business enterprises secretly of course. As the Republic of Rome grew in power and prestige, the city of Rome began to suffer from the effects of corruption, greed and the over-reliance on foreign slave labor (The current system of reliance upon cheap foreign labor with connection to the Corporatist/capitalist economies of the west).

Gangs of unemployed Romans, put out of work by the influx of slaves brought in through territorial conquests, hired themselves out as thugs to do the bidding of whatever wealthy Senator would pay them. The wealthy elite of the city, the Patricians (The wealthy Corporate /Capitalist elite of today), became ever richer at the expense of the working lower class, the Plebeians (The common citizenry).

Also, Governors gradually began accepting bribes and other cash and goods from wealthy land owners and merchants for state contract deals etc. Which in the end this sense of greed reached such a level which ultimately gave the ambitious tyrant Cesar the opportunity whereby using the gold and wealth of Crassus (whom in today's standards would be considered a wealthy/Corporate Capitalist).

Which him self was a corrupt wealthy merchant to bribe and buy his way in to the Senate and thus as history has shown...Enabling Cesar, to go as far as not only becoming the ruler of Rome...But inevitably to destroy the Roman Constitutional Republic, and plunge Rome in to centuries of Authoritarian/Totalitarian and oppressive rule...Which in the end brought about the total collapse and destruction of that once great civilization.

Now if we look upon our own times, over the past century. We will see that just as in ancient Rome, Greece and China etc. Suppressive, totalitarian and authoritarian states have only been able to come in to power when assisted or aided by the wealthy Corporate/Capitalist elite. Lets for example look at President Obama, would he have been able to reach the levels and heights which he now holds if it were not for the backing of billion-er Capitalists and Corporatists such as George Soros and others like him?.

Or how about the many financial contributions which were made to his campaign by multi Billion Dollar Corporaates such as to name a few: JPMorgan Chase & Co, GOOGLE INC. NETPAC , Citibank (Citigroup Inc), Time Warner/Comcast Corp, Sidley Austin LLP etc. etc. After all are the mentioned Corporations not the Crassus's of our time?.

So if we do not look upon history and learn from the mistakes made by as I have shown the great civilizations of the ancient world such as Rome, Greece etc. Then we today are in grave danger of repeating their mistakes and thus we face the very same fate which they ultimately had succumbed to, which is the total collapse and destruction of those once great civilizations.

CHAPTER

Two

THE INSPIRATION BEHIND
PROLETARIATISM THEORY

"So long as the Commercial sector or the world of business and finance remains with in its own respective boundaries. It can bring prosperity, productivity and a strong economy to society. However once it spills over in to the world of politics or even religion. The inevitable outcome is almost always corruption of these institutions."

-Darius Radmanesh

My theory " Proletariatism " is a political ideological tool or element which is specifically designed for one purpose. So to cement and safeguard the core principles and values which exist with in any free state, now rather it be a Constitutional Republic or A democracy. It dose not in any way replace or alter them. Yes one or two minor modifications are made, for the simple reason that my theory forwards a single main objective, that is cleansing the state of corruption.

However, as I have said the core principles with in the mentioned free systems, their Constitution, laws etc. remain intact. Yes, my theory excludes one group (The minority Corporate elite) with in society from being able to take part in or hold public office at any level. in order to achieve the mentioned objective which is the cleansing or removing of corruption from government.

Therefore In order to achieve this end, Such a measure is paramount and necessary, especially since the mentioned element is in effect the root and cause of the problem in the first place. Furthermore, I must stress that my theory is not in any way shape or form inspired or influenced by any leftist ideology now rather it be Marxism, Socialism or any other such entity.

In fact my theory was inspired by the term Proletarii or Proletariat, which was first referred to contrary to what many believe not by Marx or Engels but rather in the Constitution of the Roman, Republic over two thousand years before the hijacked and subverted version which was later introduced and referred to to by Karl Marx.

The term proletariat, in ancient Rome, basically referred to the masses, the general populace, those whom were free citizens but were not members of the wealthy elite...They weir the laborers and the common citizenry, whom may or may not have had any spacial skills, and whom performed most of the hard labor with in Roman society.

THE DIFFERENCE BETWEEN
PROLETARIATISM
&
MARX'S DISCTATORSHIP
OF THE PROLETARIAT

Dictatorship of the Proletariat basically refers to a certain life style which is enforced upon all members of society period with no exception.

It dose not however imply the superiority of one class or group of citizens over another, but rather it enforces the concept of a universal or single economical/social system on all citizens. Under Marxism, everyone in society are to live in accordance to a single standard. Meaning that no one is permitted to own private property or to accumulate private wealth.

However with regards to Proletariatism, this is not the case. Under Proletariatism theory the owning of private property or personal wealth is not prohibited. The only issue which is enforced is which group of citizens are able to run for, and hold public office. which are members of the Common citizen body (The majority) only. Meaning that all members of the Corporatist/Banking elite (The minority) are not.

This however dose not mean that they are not permitted to maintain thier wealth or thier commercial interests etc. On the contrary, as I have maintained time and time again, so long of course that they do so with in their respective boundaries and limits, there is no problem. Also in addition I think that it is important to point out that-

both their social and economical rights with in society are not discarded, violated or infringed upon, unlike under Marxism, only their political rights are restricted. This is of course do to the fact that any given time when the world of finance or industry has been permitted to gain access in to the realm of state.

The inevitable out come is always political corruption. A free prosperous industry and economy is good for society as a whole and is beneficial to everyone. My only reservations is that the commercial sector remains out of the countries political affairs..That's it, plain and simple. In this aspect my theory is very unique and novel. Also it is not in any way a economically based theory, such as capitalist or Marxist/Socialist systems. But rather that its core principle as I have stated is purely political and socially based.

its sole objective is to put in to retrospect which group of citizens should have the ultimate say and control over the affairs of state...Rather then legislating and dictating policies and laws made by the minority to be forced upon the the majority which only serves the interests of a minor section of society...

It makes it possible whereby the fate and lives of the majority is in effect placed back in to their own control and hands....By transferring the power and control of the state over to the common/ordinary citizens with in society (The majority) from the power and influence of the elitist minority whom push forward legislation and other laws so to forward their own business and financial interests at the expense of infringing upon, the freedoms, rights the interests of the majority which are the common ordinary citizens..

PROLETARIATISM
"Returning government back to the people"

Proletariatism, is the concept of a principled statesman driven system of government which is overseen exclusively by elected members of the common working class citizenry.

It is unlike the present day political apparatus we now find in the United states wherein the main focus is placed primarily on party politics, lobbyists and big corporate money, or as in other Socialist governments where the main emphases is on economic class struggle with their false and failed attempt at fairness and redistribution of wealth.

Proletariatism, is very unique in comparison with these traditional systems mentioned in that its core principle is neither party politics driven, nor economically driven like in the Capitalist/Socialist systems. Proletariatism, is a system of government which aims to foster and forward the joint activism of the working class majority allowing them the ability to become more involved in maters of state as they become individual candidates running for public office at local, state and national levels.

Proletaritaism, is in fact not a political movement, doctrine, ideology or party. It is a proactive political principle, element and ideological tool which can be easily adapted and implemented into a pre-existing system of any free state, be it a Democracy or a Republic. When a Democracy or a Republic utilizes Proletariatism, all pre-existing Constitutional laws and principles remain in place, intact and unchanged.

There are only two main modifications made to present systems with the adapting of Proletariatism, one is who will be allowed to run as a candidate and hold office, the other deals with funding. In the first case, dealing with who are allowed to run as a candidate and hold office, a change is made as to which group, class or citizen body are permitted to hold or run for public office as active elected participants in there countries politics and government .

When Proletariatism, is adapted only those citizens who are of the Proletariat, the common working class citizenry, which includes but is not limited to farmers, factory workers, welders, builders, plumbers, electricians, small business owners, professors, school teachers and so on, are allowed to hold any political office.

Only members from this group of citizens are permitted to run for public office to thus become active members of there countries politics. Whereby citizens who belong to the wealthy, elitist groups, or upper class, the minority Capitalists, consisting of Industrialists, Bankers, large manufacturers, Corporations, etc. are prohibited from ever running for or holding public office at any level.

They are also prohibited from taking any part what-so-ever in the affairs of there government either directly, by running for public office, or indirectly, making any form of financial contribution to a political campaign or any other government department, agency or body, be it at any level of government, local, state or national.

Under Proletariatism, while the wealthy are in every way prohibited from taking any level of participation in there countries government and politics, their wealth, positions, rights as a citizen, their freedoms and liberties are not molested, nor are they forced to pay higher tax rate then the rest of the populous.

They may pursue their drive to increase their holdings privately only. They are simply prohibited from taking any active roll in there country's government and politics. These measures are put in place to protect and safeguard the freedoms, liberties and the overall well being of the majority the Proletariat, the common average citizen, against the greed and Progressive advancement of the Capitalists through corruption of government.

The second element of Proletariatism deals with funding of campaigns.

Under this system, all political campaigns and candidates running for public office at all levels are prohibited from utilizing any form of second or third party financial donations or contributions for their campaign. Furthermore, candidates are also prohibited from using any of there own personal finances or monetary assists for campaigning as well.

This is a measure put in place to prevent corruption, by preventing criminal elements, foreign intrigues or Capitalists, from being able to influence the success of any campaign whereby placing an elected official under obligation indebted to them, consequently enabling the influence of legislation.

Under Proletariatism, funding for all political campaigns is provided by the state in equal amounts. Whereby all candidates are given equal sums of capital for this purpose, regardless of a candidates social or financial standing or statues.

This is done so that the success of a candidates run for office is no longer dependent on a candidates financial limitations, but rather the candidates desire to serve, his/her character, merits and abilities. It is also a means of making it possible for the average American man or women from the common working class Proletariat majority, to be able to run for public office.

This eliminates the ability of the wealthy Capitalists and other elitist groups from domineering, monopolizing and unjustly commandeering Democracies and Republics for their own greedy purposes such as we are now experiencing in America and around the world.

CHAPTER

THREE

Corporate Capitalists
&
the value of a human being

When we look at America's current political and economical crises, the down turn, the rapidly declining quality of America's health care system, etc. what do we see?..answer..the consequence of pure Corporate Capitalism or Corporate Elitism.

You may be asking, so what's wrong with Corporatism?. Well, when within a society the values and principles of morality, family, friendship, honor, traditions, honesty etc. are instead replaced with only the greedy pursuit and drive for financial gain and profit at all cost, when even humanity and the value of human life is judged and determined not by the principle that all life, regardless of race, gender, social or financial standing or even age and condition of health, but rather is measured based on ones social or monetary value and position, then Pure Capitalism, Socialist Capitalism rules.

member of the impoverished or so-called lower or working middle class the common man the (Proletariat), or if you are an elderly, disabled or handicapped person no longer able to contribute to society, then you are perceived not as a human being having the God given and natural right to life, but instead are viewed as simply a worthless sponge or parasite, a burden upon societies financial and material recourse's. Consequently, at the whim of those in power, you can be deemed as unworthy of life and that you do not deserve to exist.

This view, this perception, is a direct attribute, a consequence of, greedy, poisonous, Corporatist values and ideologies which has for far to long now been embedded into the fabric of American society, in that we are being taught to not show any respect, courtesy, compassion or charity to the weaker more vulnerable members of society, members such as the elderly, the impoverished, etc. We are taught instead to shun them away and look upon them with disdain and contempt.

18

In a society whereby Corporate elitism, has essentially infiltrated and ultimately replaced the political state, with a Corporate/economical system. In such a society the common ordinary citizen is no longer valued or viewed as a person or human being by the Corporatist ruling elite, but rather you are looked upon as a commodity or an object. Ones value is measured or determined solely based on your financial or monetary worth to the corporate system.

The Corporate elite, have been very cleaver in being able to subversively deceive and manipulate the public to turning their backs upon the weak, the elderly, the disabled and handicapped, by presenting these citizens as free loaders, those who do not contribute to the good of society, they don't pull there wait, or they are simply lazy and worthless etc and are therefore a burden upon societies financial and material resources.

They have been able to do so, by very subtly over a period of time, injecting this view into our subconsciousness, after a while even the most kindest, most God fearing charitable members of society gradually begin to succumb to this point of view and perception. This is without question a pure case of subversive social engineering or Subversive Desensitization(Brainwashing) to the point they have been very successful indeed.

They have been able to sell there poisonous views by marketing themselves as being concerned for the overall or collective well being and interests of society. They utilize this outer mask allowing them to conceal there true objective and agenda, keeping it hidden from the people.

However make no mistake, their interest is not the well being of the people within society, with you and me, but rather to insure that every citizen provides them (The Corporate elite) with capital/material and political profit and gain. What fate befalls the populace is of no importance or consequence.

The Majority & The minority

All of the most important institutions in America, be they our educational, government or the health care system, are all being controlled and influenced entirely by a very small portion of citizens, (the minority) the SO-CALLED elite, the Corporate Capitalists.

So who are these people? They are the very wealthy, rich and super rich, who's only objective and interest is exclusively the pursuit of hording of wealth, political power and self advancement...period!. They feel no remorse, they have no reservations as to how they accumulate their wealth or by what means they achieve this objective.

All this while the majority, which are the common people, the middle class workers, the ordinary average citizens in society (the Proletariat), the very group of citizens whom do all the hard work, fight in all the wars, those whom when the economy takes adown-turn are the ones who suffer and sacrifice the most, in short, the very backbone a life blood of America. Their views and concerns are pushed aside, ignored and discarded.

It is the coomon man whom has very little or no say in the affairs and governance of the country. Now many may argue that this is not true, that in America, the majority are in fact direct participants in there countries political affairs. They are of course referring to the peoples ability to vote in support of candidates running for public office either on a local, state or federal levels etc.

which, they believe, consequently gives them a say as to how the country is governed. Well, this is in reality nothing of the sort. It is all an illusion, a false pretense of having a say in America's government and political affairs.

People are permitted to take part in elections to give them a false sense of patriotism and security, however many in America are becoming fully aware that this is no more then a farce and deception, that regardless of what or how the people may vote, it is irrelevant and of very little or no consequence.

It is becoming more and more clear that no matter what citizens do through elections and in politics, the agenda and objective has already been chosen and put into effect regardless of what the people want, think or say.

The common man (the majority) have been for far to long victims of the lies and deceptions of the Corporate elite. They have for far to long been prayed upon by greedy Corporatists, whom in there ever increasing hunger for more wealth and power, have sucked and drained the very life and blood from the Common man.

Now we are to the point where the common citizen, the working class can no longer afford to live. Many Americans today are loosing there jobs and homes. They are finding it more and more difficult to put food on the table or to clothe and support there families. And so, out of desperation, in order to survive, many Americans are left with no choice or alternative but to seek assistance from what ever government programs or resources are available...welfare, forced welfare.

One final point regarding the elections process in the united states today. It makes no difference which candidate or party the people support and cast their vote for. Ultimately the men and women whom are selected by the political parties (All parties in question) and presented to the people as candidates. Are in fact chosen from members of the Corporate/Business elite.

Regardless as I have said which party or group they represent. Furthermore, the political party's in America, with out exception have at some point or another been infiltrated and subverted by the Corporate elite. Therefore no matter which party the people may support, in the end the Corporatist agenda is still pushed forward according to plan with out any complications.

Political parties in a sense are the bridges between the corporations and the state, whereby the Corporate elite utilise so to gain entry in to the halls of government. Political party's essentially have been reduced to being nothing more then lobbyists for the Corporate elite, forwarding their Corporatist/globalist agenda.

Now lets say that he will be running on the Republican ticket. Ok, then Lets say he gets elected as president. Now you know who's policies Mr. Joe, will be pushing though and enforcing? not yours or mine that's for darn sure...No sir...He will do exactly what he is told by the Republican party committee...PERIOD!

And you want to know why?, because if he (Mr. Joe) chooses to do things his way and totally discard the will of his party...Guess what?...Coming next term the Republican party will withdraw their support and endorsement from him and will not nominate and back his candidacy.

Also not to mention any and all legislation which he may try and push though in both Congress and the Senate will be automatically ignored and discarded by all Republican members of Congress and the Senate....Plain and simple. You see, right here lies the core dilemma and cause of Americas, many problems and issues.

Because we the people for far to long have been living under the false perception or should I say (Delusional perception) that all we need to do is to elect the right candidate etc or back the right party....WRONG!.

Corporatists & The Welfare State

We have witnessed how over the years America, once the greatest and most advanced Industrial country in the world, has been gradually transformed from being a producing society to becoming a society of consumers and consequently into the welfare state of today.

Now how could this have happened many may ask? America's ever increasing decline in industry and production, also its transformation into becoming almost entirely a welfare state has been by no means an accident, but rather it has been very much intentional.

This process was in fact initiated during Bill Clinton's presidency. Whereby in 1993 when he signed off on the North American free trade agreement and the general agreement on trade and tariffs, otherwise known as NAFTA/GATT, he quite literally slashed the economic throat of the United States. America, has been hemorrhaging jobs to foreign countries such as Communist China, India and South American countries ever since.

One other important contributor to forwarding the Globalist/Corporate agenda is the 2012 Republican presidential candidate Mitt Romney. Whom through his financial company Bain Capital, invested in a series of firms which specialised in relocated jobs done by American, workers to new facilities located in low-wage countries such as China and India.

Bain is a private equity and venture capital firm but also delves into long/short public equity, credit products and global macro HEDGE FUNDS with offices in Boston, London, New York, Munich, Chicago, Hong Kong, Tokyo, Shanghai and Mumbai. Bain Capital has invested in over 200 companies since its inception.

The firms current assets under management total $78 billion. Which clearly places it on the rank of being one of the top leading global conglomerate Corporates in the world. In addition to Mr. Romney, one other notable high profiled individual which played a fundamental role in forwarding this objective was non other then president George W Bush.

Both Mr. Bush, and his family are what you could call the cream of crop with in the globalist Corporate elite circles. During the duration of George W Bush, as president, from the time he was elected the country lost more than 2 million manufacturing jobs since he was elected. In the state of Ohio alone, suffered the loss of 270,000 manufacturing jobs during his administration.

Do to George W Bushes policies, The economic crisis which was the result, raised questions about why the White House had so strongly endorsed the outsourcing of U.S. jobs to cheap overseas labor markets. Basically George Bushes actions boil down to one fundamental fact concerning party politics in America today.

Which is that its not about the Democratic party or the Republican party etc. Because ultimately both or even possibly all parties in the United states have been at some level subverted or infiltrated by the Corporate elite. Also its not about individual candidates either, now rather it be George W Bush, Clinton (Bill or Hillary) or any other Candidate.

Most Americans, believe that ..." hey If one official doesn't do their job right then we will just vote him or her out and elect someone else ". With out realising it we are simply continuing the same cycle and statuesque over and over and over again with out ever at any time changing or altering the policy, objective and direction of the statuesque.

No matter whom we elect regardless of which party the candidate or Candidates may be representing, In the end its always business as usual and nothing changes. You know why?, because its not down to, or dependent upon individual candidates, because ultimately even if a candidate is truly sincere and honest and dedicated to the cause of upholding our countries sacred document the United states Constitution and the over all well being and best interests of the American people.

In the end its not about what a elected official wants or not, but rather its about what policies and objectives his or her party wish to push forward, you see what I am saying here?. Lets say for example we the people back and support a specific candidate, lets call him Mr. Joe, to run in the presidential elections.

Now lets say that he will be running on the Republican ticket. Ok, then Lets say he gets elected as president. Now you know who's policies Mr. Joe, will be pushing though and enforcing? not yours or mine that's for darn sure...No sir...He will do exactly what he is told by the Republican party committee...PERIOD!

And you want to know why?, because if he (Mr. Joe) chooses to do things his way and totally discard the will of his party...Guess what?...Coming next term the Republican party will withdraw their support and endorsement from him and will not nominate and back his candidacy.

Also not to mention any and all legislation which he may try and push though in both Congress and the Senate will be automatically ignored and discarded by all Republican members of Congress and the Senate....Plain and simple. You see, right here lies the core dilemma and cause of Americas, many problems and issues.

Because we the people for far to long have been living under the false perception or should I say (Delusional perception) that all we need to do is to elect the right candidate etc or back the right party....WRONG!.

Now as for the parties them selves...Well..they regardless of which one you support or back, in turn are as I have explained before, have been reduced to being nothing more then Lobbyists for the Corporate elite.

forwarding their globalist objectives and agendas period, so no matter which candidate or party the people support. Ultimately nothing changes and the Corporatist continue with forwarding their objection with relative comfort and ease.

This is mainly because the people wont have any other option at there disposal, and thus not wanting to loose whatever assistance, both financially or in housing, given to them by the government they will submit freely to bondage. They simply bow there heads in submission and accept whatever laws or demands imposed upon them.

Another major factor in the peoples unquestionable obedience in a welfare state is that in such circumstances the people become demoralized, they loose all self respect and consequently also any inner strength, ability, or even the desire to fight back.

They truly become no more then subdued voiceless sheep, placing there lives and the lives of there loved ones entirely in the hands of their benefactors, their Capitalist masters.

2- To transform and utilise the unemployed and unskilled masses in the mentioned third world economies and transform them in to armies of cheap and low maintenance labor force. Slave labor force, the very fate which awaits the peoples of all nations. This is a global/universal objective and designated for not just one country or society but rather it is the ultimate objective which is to be implemented in every country in the world.

3- To increase the number of unemployed in America. By doing so they are forcing the people more and more to become dependent on government welfare. Therefore the Corporate elite, will not have to pay the required standard of pay in America.

While at the same time increasingly transform Americans, from being what Corporatists perceive as a costly work force into a purely consuming one as they purchase and consume the many cheaply produced and low quality products and goods produced in the many industries owned and operated in foreign countries using cheap foreign labor.

This process is not just being implemented in the United states. But rather it is as we speak also being put in to place in all major western countries across Europe as well.

The purpose behind such measures unlike what many may perceive as simply being A commercially based motive. Is in fact the first steps in forwarding a much more sinister and evil objective, put in to motion by the worlds many Corporate elitist groups, which its implications upon the worlds population will be unimaginable and catastrophic .

The objective in question is to bring about or establish upon the earth a universal/one world system which will not be as many have mistakenly assumed, a political system. But rather it will be a purely economical one whereby all ordinary and common members of the citizenry will be viewed and treated as no better then slaves or commodities very much like cattle or live stock.

Whereby their only worth and value to the system and their worthiness to live will be measured purely based on their labor and monetary worth. All others such as the handicapped, the elderly, the disabled, the terminally ill and also the poor, or anyone else whom is not able to fulfil their expected tasks or is perceived as simply a burden upon societies financial and material recourse's, will simply be systematically and indiscriminately done a way with or eliminated.

 This new world system or order, will be non other then state Capitalism/ Socialism or State Corporatism on a universal scale. Universal Socialism will be when when essentially the political state in every country in the world has been replaced with a economical one. This universal Socialism is in effect the Communism envisioned by Karl Marx.

> After all the core principle of Socialism is entirely economically based....The concept of state Capitalism, contrary to what many believe to be the brain child of Marx, was in fact a theory contrived by Charles Fourier.

Whereby he advocated the political powers of the state to be done a way with and instead to reduce government to holding no more then economical administrative authorities, hence (State Capitalism). Also, I think that it is appropriate to mention that Communism, contrary to what many believe has never existed neither in the former Soviet Union China and Cuba today etc

Because all of the mentioned states are and were Socialist states. Communism with the small (c) is in fact the ultimate Utopian goal or universal objective of state Capitalism or (Universal Socialism). And communism with the large (C) refers to the real life or phesycal form of Communism by WW2 era Marxists. Which is to replace all political states of the world in to a single Economical state, governed by a single elitist body comprised of all the major Corporations of the world.

At this level all civil governments, laws and also civil and social rights and liberties are cast aside, and are no longer relevant or viable. A persons right to life or the right to exist, as pointed out before, will be based solely on and, will depend exclusively on a persons economical and monetary worth to the system, period.

CHAPTER

FOUR

In my view society is like a family and the state (Head of that family) and the commercial sector is (The Corporate). These two bodies the state and Corporate are two separate bodies with two totally different and distinctly separate tasks and objectives. The task of the state is to protect, safeguard and ensure the stability, freedoms, liberties and the over all well being of its citizens (Its family) above all else indiscriminately or with out prejudice.

The commercial sector on the other hand, has only one objective and purpose and that is, capital profit first foremost. Now with regards to Corporates, if for whatever reason the profit margins of a corporation or industry is shown to be low or is on the decline, It must take all measures necessary so to maintain a minimum overhead.

In such a scenario one of the first acts to be enforced is to cut costs which among other things also entails the laying off of a number of its personal or employees. This is done with out any consideration whatsoever being made as to what impact such a measure will have or make on the lives of these individuals and there families.

After all the bottom line here is to maintain profit margin at all costs with out exception, hence the old saying " This is business not personal " .

Now lets turn our attention to the state or (Head Of Family) whereby society is like that of a family and its citizens are its members and the state its head. Within a household, when times are hard and financial recourse's are low dose the head of that family start throwing out members of his or her family in order to cut costs? of course not.

After all the well being and the interests of all family members take precedence over all else, this includes financial interests. So, how can we then trust members from the Commercial sector (Corporate Capitalists/Businessmen/women) whom occupy various prominent positions within government to uphold and safeguard the well being and overall interests of the people indiscriminately and with out prejudice?.

When their entire purpose and sole reasoning for entering politics in the first place was to increase and further there capital and monetary gain?. After all these are businessmen and women (NOT!) statesmen and their only sole interest is their own personal financial gain, and NOT the overall interest of the ordinary citizen body?.

Because ultimately, When a statesmen applies him or her self to a task concerning matters of state...He or she dose so with what I call a (Social/Civil Perception) mindset, meaning that they view any given issue or situation on such matters with a mined set which takes in to account and consideration all social and civil aspects or elements with in society. However, When an individual whom is by profession a businessman or woman, is applied to the same tasks.

Their view point or perception regarding society defers greatly, such individuals whom have devoted most of, or even all of there time to the world of commerce and finance. Whereby there only objective and interest has been exclusively the condoning of business and generating of capital profit. When such individuals are then placed at the helm of government,

such perception is in turn implemented in to the political apparatus of any given state as well...Whereby society is no longer measured based on the elements of civil and social standards or principles but rather is measured in Dollars and Cents. The human or civil element in such scenarios are void and are not taken in to account and are not existent.

Only the profit margin is considered. And this is why a business man or woman must NOT! ever be permitted to hold any position within the state. And that the halls of government MUST! only be filled with honorable and capable statesmen and women whom have absolutely no ties whatsoever or interests with the Commercial/Business sector.

Making a profit is very well and fin, so long as it is in the private or Commercial sector and not in politics. Because once the objective of For the simple fact that In the world of business if a bad business decision is made, then only the businessman suffers the down fall. However, if a business deal falls through which was made by the state. Then the entire citizenry will feel its implications and suffer its consequences.

Some argue that if we do not select or elect our leaders from the wealthy Corporatist/Business class, then the only other option or alternative would be to elect those whom are either Community organisers (Leftist/Marxist individuals or groups), men or women of the cloth or lawyers?. To such statements I my answer is that why must we either submit and bow before the Corporatist elite, or to Marxists, religious leaders or attorneys?.

Why not instead we place our faith and hope in the hands of the very people whom have been from the beginning the builders and pioneers of our great country. They whom have fought in and have died in every war America, has ever taken part in right from her conception, the common citizenry.

Men and women such as the hard working blue blooded American farmer, fire fighter, police man, lumber jack, carpenter, builder, factory worker, school teachers, College professors and soldiers etc.

The common citizenry or common man (The majority) These are the true builders and life blood of America, therefore it is these whom also should be at the helm of our government, and also to have a decisive and final say as to how our country is governed, and not the so-called elitists, the wealthy Corporatists (The minority).

It is a real outrage and tragedy whereby in our society today, the terms Common and working man have become synonymous with leftist ideologies of Socialism, Marxism or Communism.

When in fact not one of the mentioned degenerate institutions of the left have even in the most remote since contributed to addressing the many plights, struggles and hardships which the Common man has been forced to face and endure.

It is becoming more and more clear that no matter what citizens do through elections and in politics, the agenda and objective has already been chosen and put into effect regardless of what the people want, think or say.

If any thing, such a stigma has in fact increased the difficulties of the common ordinary citizen, simply for the reason that no one with in a free society will ever admit publicly of being a member of the common citizenry or the working class for the mentioned reasons.

CHAPTER

FIVE

AMERICA A CORPORATE CAPITALIST, NOT A LAISSEZ-FAIRE, FREE MARKET SYSTEM.

I think that it is important that we first understand what a free market laissez-fairesystem or economy is. Basically the core principle of the laissez-fairesy, system is the minimizing of government influence and interference in a societies economy, whereby governments roll in the economy is broken down and restricted in to only two points:

1- First two enforce the laws which protect contracts and civil order.
2- To maintain low taxation and very minimum to no interference in the countries economical affairs by the state.
That's it, these are the only active rolls which the state, is permitted in taking part under a true laissez-fairesy system.

laissez-faire, (French: "allow to do"), policy of minimum governmental interference in the economic affairs of individuals and society.

The origin of the term is uncertain, but folklore suggests that it is derived from the answer Jean-Baptiste Colbert, controller general of finance under King Louis XIV of France, received when he asked industrialists what the government could do to help business: ....the reply was... "Leave us alone."

The doctrine of laissez-faire is usually associated with the economists known as Physiocrats, who flourished in France from about 1756 to 1778..

Belief in laissez-faire was a popular view during the 19th century; its proponents cited the assumption in classical economics of a natural economic order as support for their faith in unregulated individual activity.

The British economist John Stuart Mill was responsible for bringing this philosophy into popular economic usage in his Principles of Political Economy (1848), in which he set forth the arguments for and against government activity in economic affairs.

Laissez-faire was a political as well as an economic doctrine. The pervading theory of the 19th century was that the individual, pursuing his own desired ends, would thereby achieve the best results for the society of which he was a part.

The function of the state was to maintain order and security and to avoid interference with the initiative of the individual in pursuit of his own desired goals. But laissez-faire advocates nonetheless argued that government had an essential role in enforcing contracts as well as ensuring civil order (ONLY).

Now lets draw our attention to what was called the " Hamiltonian economic program " which then became known as " The American School of economics " AKA " Capitalism " America's current economic system. After examining all of the mentioned policies and systems we will be able to clearly conclude that, the economical system which Hamilton had implemented in to American was any thing but a free laissez-faire market system.

On the contrary, we will clearly see that it was in fact a system which covertly forwarded a system which in time would establish or bring about in America, a very large and powerful centralised Federal government. Which would eventually over ride and suppress the sovereignty's and rights of the states.

In addition, we shall also see that Hamilton's system was nothing more then a deceptive and subversive tactic in establishing a powerful government which would ultimately be not a political state but rather one governed and controlled exclusively by the Corporatist and Banking elite.

Whereby the halls of government would not be filled with capable, honorable, courageous and virtuous men and women both selected and elected from the ordinary common citizenry. But rather it would be occupied by men and women of the Corporate elite.

Forwarding only their capital gains, profits and interests and not the interests of the nation as a whole. A tragedy which has continued to the very present day. As clearly shown in the documents bellow, Hamilton's system places great emphases primarily on the power and control of government in all economical affairs .

The Hamiltonian economic program was the set of measures that were proposed by American Founding Father and 1stSecretary of the Treasury Alexander Hamilton in three notable reports and implemented by Congress during George Washington's first administration.

-First Report on Public Credit - pertaining to the assumption of federal and state debts and finance of the United States government.

-Second Report on Public Credit - pertaining to the establishment of a National Bank.

-Report on Manufactures - pertaining to the policies to be followed to encourage manufacturing and industry within the United States.

The First Report on the Public Credit was one of three major reports on fiscal and economic policy submitted byAmerican Founding Father and first United States Treasury Secretary Alexander Hamilton on the request of Congress. The report analyzed the financial standing of the United States of America and made recommendations to reorganize the national debt and to establish the public credit.

Commissioned by the House of Representatives on September 21, 1789, the Report was presented on January 9, 1790, at the second session of the First US Congress. The 40,000 word document called for full federal payment at face value to holders of government securities ("Redemption") and the national government to assume funding of all state debt ("Assumption").

The Second Report on the Public Credit also referred to as The Report on a National Bank was the second of three influential reports on fiscal and economic policy delivered to Congress by Secretary of the Treasury Alexander Hamilton.

The Report, submitted on December 14, 1790, called for the establishment of a central bank, its primary purpose to expand the flow of legal tender by monetizing the national debt through the issuance of federal bank notes. Modeled on the Bank of England, this privately held, but publicly funded institution would also serve to process revenue fees and perform fiscal duties for the federal government-

Secretary Hamilton regarded the bank as indispensable to producing a stable and flexible financial system.

The ease with which Federalists advanced legislation to incorporate the bank impelled agrarian opposition hostile to Hamilton 's emerging economic nationalism. Resorting to constitutional arguments, Representative James Madison challenged Congress's broad authority to grant charters of incorporation under the"necessary and proper" clause of the US Constitution, and charging Hamilton with violating a literal or strict constructionist interpretation of the founding document.

Despite Madison's objections, the legislation to form the First Bank of the United States passed, without amendment, in the House by a vote of 37-20 on February 2, 1791, endowed with a twenty-year charter

The American School of economics, represented the legacy of Alexander Hamilton, who in his Report on Manufactures, argued that the U.S. could not become fully independent until it was self-sufficient in all necessary economic products.
Frank Bourgin's 1989 study of the Constitutional Convention shows that direct government involvement in the economy was intended by the Founders.

The goal, most forcefully articulated by Hamilton, was to ensure that dearly won political independence was not lost by being economically and financially dependent on the powers and princes of Europe.

The creation of a strong central government able to promote science, invention, industry and commerce, was seen as an essential means of promoting the general welfare and making the economy of the United

States strong enough for them to determine their own destiny. A number of programs by the federal government undertaken in the period prior to the Civil War gave shape and substance to the American School.

Central policies

The American School included three cardinal policy points:

> **1**-Support industry: The advocacy of protectionism, and opposition to free trade - particularly for the protection of "infant industries" and those facing import competition from abroad. Examples: Tariff of 1816 and Morrill Tariff.

2-Create physical infrastructure: Government finance of internal improvements to speed commerce and develop industry. This involved the regulation of privately held infrastructure, to ensure that it meets the nation's needs. Examples: Cumberland Road and Union Pacific Railroad

3-Create financial infrastructure: A government sponsored National Bank to issue currency and encourage commerce. This involved the use of sovereign powers for the regulation of credit to encourage the development of the economy, and to deter speculation. Examples: First Bank of the United States, Second Bank of the United States, and National Banking Act.

Henry C. Carey, a leading American economist and adviser to Abraham Lincoln, in his book Harmony of Interests, displays two additional points of this American School economic philosophy that distinguishes it from the systems of Adam Smith or Karl Marx:

> **1**-Government support for the development of science and public education through a public 'common' school system and investments in creative research through grants and subsidies.

> **2**-Rejection of class struggle, in favor of the "Harmony of Interests" between: owners and workers, farmer and manufacturers, the wealthy class and the working class.[18]

Executive Opposition to the American System: The Jacksonians.

Opposition to the economic nationalism embodied by Henry Clay's "American System" came primarily from the Democratic Party of Andrew Jackson, Martin van Buren, and James K. Polk. These three presidents styled themselves as the peoples' politicians, seeking to protect both the agrarian frontier culture and the strength of the Union. Jackson in particular, the founder of the movement, held an unflinching commitment to what he viewed as the sanctity of the majority opinion.

In his first annual message to Congress, Jackson proclaimed that "the first principle of our system [is] that the majority govern".[22] This ideology governed Jackson's actions throughout his presidency, and heavily influenced his protégé Martin van Buren as well as the final Jacksonian president, James K. Polk.

This commitment to the majority and to the voiceless came in direct conflict with many elements of the American System. The Jacksonian presidents saw key tenets of the American System, including the support for the Second Bank of the United States and advocacy of protectionist tariffs, as serving moneyed or special interests rather than the majority of Americans.

The Jacksonians opposed other elements of Clay's ideology, including support for internal infrastructural improvements, on the grounds that they represented governmental overstretch as well. Several key events, legislative conflicts, and presidential vetoes shaped the substantive opposition to the American System.

The Second Bank of the United States and the Bank War

The first and most well-known battle between Jacksonians and Clay focused on the struggle over renewing the charter of the Second Bank of the United States. In Andrew Jackson's first annual message to Congress in 1829, he declared that " both the constitutionality and the expediency of the law creating this bank are well questioned by a large portion of our fellow-citizens, and it must be admitted by all that it has failed in the great end of establishing a uniform and sound currency".

He further attacked the proponents of renewing the bank's charter, scathingly referring to the "stockholders" seeking a renewal of their "privileges".

This rhetoric, portraying the supporters of the bank as privileged individuals, and claiming the opposition of "a large portion of our fellow-citizens" crystallizes Jackson's majoritarian distaste for the special interest serving economic nationalism embodied in the American System. Jackon's Secretary of the Treasury Roger B.

Taney effectively summed up Jackson's opposition to the Second Bank of the United States: ""It is a fixed principle of our political institutions to guard against the unnecessary accumulation of power over persons and property in any hands. And no hands are less worthy to be trusted with it than those of a moneyed corporation".

The two sides of the debate became even more starkly defined as a result of the actions of Second Bank President Nicholas Biddle and Henry Clay himself. Upon hearing of Jackson's distaste for his bank, Biddle immediately set about opening new branches of the bank in key political districts in hopes of manipulating Congressional opinion

> Although this action indeed helped acquire the votes necessary to pass the bill in Congress, it enraged Jackson. Jackson saw this manipulation as clear evidence of the penchant of a national bank to serve private, non-majoritarian interests.
> Henry Clay's American System supported the necessity for central institutions to "take an activist role in shaping and advancing the nation's economic development"

The bank thus fit well into Clay's worldview, and he took advantage of Biddle's manipulation in order to pass the renewal bill through Congress, despite expecting Jackson's inevitable veto. Clay hoped that when Jackson vetoed the bill, it would more clearly differentiate the two sides of the debate which Clay then sought to use to his advantage in running for president. With battle lines set, Jackson's majoritarian opposition to the Second Bank of the United States helped him be elected to a second term.

The Tariff Question

The question of protective tariffs championed by the American System proved one of the trickiest for Jacksonian presidents. Tariffs disproportionately benefited the industrial interests of the North while causing great injury to the trade-dependent agrarian South and West. As a result, the issue proved extremely divisive to the nation's unity, something Jacksonian presidents sought to protect at all costs.

> The Jacksonian presidents, particularly the southern-born Jackson, had to be extremely cautious when lowering tariffs in order to maintain their support in the North.

However, the tariffs indeed represented an economic nationalism that benefited only a portion of the American electorate, not the majority. This ran strongly contrary to Jacksonian ideals. In the end, despite Northern objections, both President Jackson and President Polk lowered tariffs. Jackson reformed the Tariff of 1828 (also known as the Tariff of Abominations) by radically reducing rates in the Tariff of 1832.

This helped stave off the Southern nullification crisis, in which Southern states refused to enact the tariff, and threatened secession if faced with governmental coercion. The bill that reduced the Tariff of 1828 was co-authored by Henry Clay in a desperate attempt to maintain national unity. Polk, on the other hand, in his characteristically efficient way, managed to push through significant tariff reductions in the first 18 months of his term.

Only members from this group of citizens are permitted to run for public office to thus become active members of there countries politics. Whereby citizens who belong to the wealthy, elitist groups, or upper class, the minority Capitalists, consisting of Industrialists, Bankers, large manufacturers, Corporations, etc. are prohibited from ever running for or holding public office at any level.

Opposition to Government-Financed Internal Improvements.

The final bastion of Jacksonian opposition to Clay's American System existed in relation to the use of government funds to conduct internal improvements.

The Jacksonian presidents feared that government funding of such projects as roads and canals exceeded the mandate of the federal government and should not be undertaken.Van Buren believed very strongly that " the central government, unlike the states, had no obligation to provide relief or promote the general welfare.

This stance kept faith with the tenets of Jeffersonian republicanism, notably its agrarianism and strict constructionism, to which van Buren was heir". As heir to the legacy of Van Buren and Jackson, Polk was similarly hostile to internal improvement programs, and used his presidential veto to prevent such projects from reaching fruition.

I think that it is also important to point out that the man whom has been proclaimed (Falsly) as the father of modern free economics Adam Smith, whos work " The Wealth Of Nations " had a profound influance on Hamilton's drafting of his economic program.

Was in fact him self a strong advocate and supporter for governments strong influence in the economy of society. A fact clearly proven in the follwoing statement whereby he also refers to the people with in society not as citizens but rather as subjects?. Which is a clear indication as to his stance and position regarding the exsesive centrelised power and authority of the state over the people.

"The subjects of every state ought to contribute towards the support of the government, as nearly as possible, in proportion to their respective abilities; that is, in proportion to the revenue which they respectively enjoy under the protection of the state"

[Adam Smith, in support of government]

Furthermore, it is also important to note that Adam Smiths stance on a poerful centrelised government drew parise and aclaim by non other then Karl Marx and Engles, the founders of Marxist Socialism.

" Smith is the (Martin) Luther of Political economy "

-Friedrich Engles

In fact so much so, that Marx's economic and philosophic manuscript of 1884 discloses the crucial importance of Adam Smiths work for his own project. The first important formation of Marx's theory, is found in Paris Notebooks of 1844. In which he divides his manuscript in three columns...

1-The wages of Labor.

2-The profit of Capital.

3-and the rent of land

Thus reproducing Smith's tripartite division of political economy. Hence Smith was a decisive influence on the development of Marx's theory whereby from the beginning to the end of his intellectual labors...Marx's vocabulary, problems and systematic intentions were highly influenced by Smiths work.

In order for us now to better understand the truth behind Hamiltons Economic program " Capitalism " and its hidden agenda. We must now turn our focus on the Hamilton him self. Basically Hamilton, was in fact a devout Monarchist, and secretly harbored strong desires to establish a Monarchical style of government in America, after our victory in the war of Independence against Britain.

However he knew very well that the American, people also not to mention many of the founding fathers such as Thomas Jefferson and Benjamin Franklin etc. would not in any way accept such a monstrosity especially since we had just achieved our independence from Britain.

So he went about contriving a secret plan in how to inject a system in to America, which would in time transform our free Republic in to just that, a Monarchical style system with a powerful centralised government. Now how did he exactly go about doing this??, he used Adam Smiths economical system as the foundation with which to build his scheme upon.

Because he was fully aware that he would not be able to achieve his objective by political means alone. He had to disguise it, in other words he needed a Trojan horse and in Smiths Wealth Of Nations, he found it. Because Smith very clearly advocated a economical system which required...no...advocated a strong government presence and involvement in a societies economy.

Thus Hamilton knew that by adapting Capitalism, as the main economical system for America, it would in time give rise to a power and strong government which in time would transform our Republican system in to a Monarchical style of government.

However under the Articles of Confederation which protected the individual rights, freedoms and soverignties of each state with a small federal government holding minimal powers. Such a scheme would have been impossible, because ultimatly in order for his plan to work it would require that the Federal government would have undisputed and dominant powers and control over all states.

So therefore he had to once and for all eliminate the Independence and safety valve of the states which was the Articles. Thus it was for this reason that he and his accomplice Madison, sat about drafting our countries current document the United States Constitution, which would do just that.

It would take away a great portion of the states powers and in time it would replace our countries Republican system of government with a Monarchical like government, and as history has shown that is exactly what happened. Bellow I have provided a number of historically documented proof and evidence which will clearly point this fact.

Thomas Jefferson, recalling a dinner conversation in 1791: "Mr. John Adams observed,..'Purge [the British] constitution of its corruption . . . and it would be the most perfect constitution ever devised by the wit of man.' Hamilton paused and said, 'Purge it of its corruption . . . and it would become an impracticable government. As it stands at present, with all its supposed defects, it is the most perfect government which ever existed.'

The "corruption" that concerned Jefferson was the allegedly excessive influence of the Executive branch over the Legislative—not necessarily anything we would regard as dishonest today. Jefferson was especially concerned about Hamilton's proposals for funding the National debt and establishing a National Bank, both means by which speculators and financiers—and legislators—could become enriched.

Jefferson envisioned America as a society based on agriculture, with the small farmer being the quintessential American. He viewed banks and long-term debt as inherently evil, or at least suspect. Hamilton, by contrast, believed that America's future lay with business, and that banks and bond markets are both necessary and beneficial.

In a 1789 letter to James Madison, Jefferson stated his famous dictum "that the earth belongs in usufruct to the living." He meant that future generations have a right to receive the benefits of the earth without impairment and, consequently, no generation has a right to impair the benefits to be transmitted to the next one.

As an application of this dictum, Jefferson concluded that debt, and particularly the National debt, should impose no obligation for more than 19 years. He believed any part of the debt that remained unpaid after that time should be extinguished—so future generations could inherit the Nation's assets debt free.

If this theory had prevailed, it would have drastically reduced the market value of Government securities, enabling the Government to pay off the debt without resorting to internal taxes, such as the whisky tax. To Hamilton and his Federalist party, Jefferson's theory was reprehensible and inconsistent with the Constitution's disapproval of laws "impairing the obligation of contracts."

" Hamilton's economic model was heavily dependent on the British example. "

-*Thomas Jefferson*

"To those steeped in this radical Whig ideology, Hamilton's system threatened to re-create the kind of government and society that many Americans thought they had destroyed in 1776. Such a hierarchical society, based on patronage connections and artificial privilege and supported by a bloated executive bureaucracy and a standing army, would in time, the destroy the integrity and independence of the republican citizenry. Hamilton's federal program, including the funding of Revolutionary debt, assuming the state debts, adopting excise taxes, establishing a standing army, and creating a national bank, seemed to be reminiscent of what Sir Robert Walpole and other ministers had done in England earlier in the century. Hamilton appeared to be using his new economic system to create a swelling phalanx of what Jefferson called 'stock-jobbers and king-jobbers' in order to corrupt Congress and build up executive power at the expense of the people in the way eighteenth-century British ministers had done."

-*Thomas Jefferson*

Hamilton argued for a large standing army not because he feared an invasion by France or England, but because he understood that the European monarchs had used such armies to intimidate their own citizens when it came to tax collection.

Evidence of this is the fact that Hamilton personally led some 15,000 conscripts into Western Pennsylvania (with George Washington) to attempt to quell the famous Whiskey Rebellion. He was eventually put in charge of the entire expedition, and rounded up two dozen tax protesters, every one of whom he wanted to hang. They were all pardoned by George Washington, however, to Hamilton's everlasting regret.

When the duplicitous Hamilton was questioned as to why he helped draft the new Constitution, he guardedly replied:

" My motives must remain in the depository of my own breast."

-*Hamilton*

And why did Hamilton make such a statement when asked this question?. Because he was fully aware of what his intentions and objectives held for America, and that they were any thing but honorable. he was fully aware that what he was pushing forward was not a system so to protect and safeguard the freedoms, rights and prosperity of America and the American people.

But rather he was setting in to motion a demonic beast which would in time so covertly and completely enslave and subjugate a nation, that it would take many many generations of Americans before they come to the realisation that they have in fact been deceived. However I fear that when such a realization dose take place, it will come very to little and very to late.

Madison, Hamiltons partner in crime was but one member of the Philadelphia Convention who secretly resented the independence of America. James Madison is considered the "father" of the US Constitution. He was heavily influenced, as were many American politicians, by the philosophy of French aristocrat Baron de Montesquieu, who believed in rule by monarchs.

Madison was also influenced by the writings of the British empiricist philosopher John Locke, who was himself "a major investor in the English slave-trade through the Royal Africa Company." Madison was vehemently opposed to state independence and pushed the Constitution to keep power well and truly out of the hands of ordinary Americans. He openly advocated an anti-republican ideology, and explained how the illiterate masses should be divided and controlled:

" Where a majority are united by a common sentiment, and have an opportunity, the rights of the minor party become insecure. In a republican government the majority, if united, have always an opportunity. The only remedy is to enlarge the sphere and thereby divide the community into so great a number of interests and parties that, in the first place, a majority will not be likely, at the same moment, to have a common interest separate from that of the whole, or of the minority; and, in the second place, that, in case they should have such an interest, they may not be so apt to unite in the pursuit of it "

-Madison

DiLorenzo's title, 18th century in its expansiveness, succinctly sums up his main theme. Thomas Jefferson supported the American Revolution in order to promote individual liberty. To secure this end, it was essential that the central government be strictly limited in its powers. America, in the Jeffersonian view, was an alliance of sovereign states, and the adoption of the Constitution, though it increased the power of the national government, did not fundamentally change this arrangement.

Alexander Hamilton disagreed. He bemoaned the limited powers given to the central government under the Articles of Confederation and continually agitated for a new scheme of authority. At the Constitutional Convention, it became clear how radical were his plans.

He favored a permanent president and senate and wanted the federal government to have the power to appoint state governors. What was behind this radical plan of centralization, fortunately rejected by the majority of the convention? DiLorenzo follows up the brilliant suggestion of Cecilia Kenyon that Hamilton was the "Rousseau of the Right."

Rousseau thought that society should be guided by the "general will," but what exactly that concept entailed has perplexed later commentators. It cannot be equated with what the majority of a certain society wishes: it is only when the people's decisions properly reflect the common good, untrammeled by faction, that the general will operates.

But if the general will need not result from straightforward voting, how is it to be determined? One answer, for which there is some textual support in Rousseau, is that a wise legislator will guide the people toward what they really want. Those who dissent will "be forced to be free." This was precisely Hamilton's view.

Government, directed by the wise such as himself, would guide the people toward what was good for them rather they wanted it or not. Clinton Rossiter, a Cornell political scientist, catalogued how some version of "the general will" appears hundreds of times in Hamilton's speeches, letters, and writings. Hamilton more pointedly than any other political thinker of his time, introduced the concept of the "public good" into American thought. (p. 23, quoting Rossiter)

CHAPTER

SIX

THE FEDERALISTS & WHAT THEY PERCIVED

TO BE THE BEST FORM OF GOVERNMENT.

Federalists believed that the country should be ruled by "best people" – educated, wealthy, public-spirited men like themselves. Such people had the time, education, and background to run the country wisely. In the words of a promonent Fedarlist John Jay Bluntly, whom was the president of Congress and Americas first Justice Of The peace:

"Those who own the country ought to govern it."

-John Jay bluntly

This was precisely Hamilton's view. Government, directed by the wise such as himself, would guide the people toward what was good for them, rather they wanted it or not. Clinton Rossiter, a Cornell political scientist, catalogued how some version of "the general will" appears hundreds of times in Hamilton's speeches, letters, and writings… Hamilton more pointedly than any other political thinker of his time, introduced the concept of the "public good" into American thought.

quoting Rossiter) Hamilton did not secure what he wanted at the Convention, and in his contributions to the Federalist Papers, he sometimes for purposes of propaganda defended the limited government that he really rejected.

But with the onset of the new government in 1789, he by no means abandoned his goal of centralized power. He had been, during the American Revolution, George Washington's military aide; and the new president appointed him secretary of the Treasury. In that capacity, he bombarded Washington with advice on interpreting the Constitution.

The powers of the central government in his view were not confined to those expressly delegated to it — far from it. The national government had also various powers "implied" by its express grants, though the logic of these implications escaped those not enamored of big government.

"'Implied powers' are powers that are not actually in the Constitution but that statists like Hamilton wish were there" (p. 26). The government also had "resulting" powers: these were not even present in the Constitution by implication but "resulted" from new situations. If, e.g., the government conquered new territory, it acquired sovereign power over it.

"'This would be rather the result from the whole mass of the government ... than a consequence of ... powers specially enumerated'" (p. 28, quoting Hamilton). As if this were not enough, Hamilton did not scruple to interpret the words of the Constitution against their plain sense.

Congress was granted the power to pass laws "necessary and proper" for its enumerated powers. To Hamilton, "necessary" meant "convenient"; what was the small matter of the dictionary to stand in the way of the public interest?

In other words, such powers should be made up, even fabricated, on the whims of politicians posing as guardians of the "public good." He [Hamilton] went on to say that any act of government is to be permitted if it is not expressly prohibited by the Constitution, something he forgot to mention in The Federalist Papers.

Thus, in his report to Washington on the constitutionality of a national bank, Hamilton held that, since Congress had the power to coin money, and in his opinion a national bank would be helpful for a monetary system, the bank passed the constitutional test. Jefferson disagreed. Regardless of whether Hamilton was right about the desirability of a bank — and Jefferson of course rejected Hamilton's view of the matter — a bank was not "necessary" and hence had no constitutional warrant.

As his opinion on the bank suggests, much of Hamilton's centralizing plans aimed at economic goals. Once more in contrast to Jefferson, he believed that the government should guide the economy. He returned to the mercantilist system famously condemned by Adam Smith in The Wealth of Nations.

> (Murray Rothbard has noted that Smith failed completely to repudiate mercantilism; nevertheless, he strongly criticized the main planks of that system.) For Hamilton, economics and politics were inextricably mixed. Here DiLorenzo follows Douglass Adair, perhaps the foremost 20th-century student of the Federalist Papers.
>
> By tying members of the business elite of the states to the new central government, in large part through their involvement in government debt, the power of the national government would be secured.
>
> "With devious brilliance, Hamilton set out, by a program of class legislation, to unite the propertied interests of the eastern seaboard into a cohesive administration party, while at the same time he attempted to make the executive dominant over the Congress by a lavish use of the spoils system." (pp. 45–46, quoting Adair)

-The economical system favored by Thomas Jefferson, and intended for America, was a free Laissez-faire economic policy and not Hamiltons big centerlised government system.

A TREATISE ON POLITICAL ECONOMY

> Thomas Jefferson had a vision for America, to establish a free Laissez-faire economic policy where people followed their own pursuits to produce a living based on their own goals and objectives, America would receive a substantial portion of it's income from agriculture and everyone would make their own possessions. In other words, Jefferson believed America should be totally self-sufficient; Jefferson was highly enthusiastic about the Traité.
>
> Even though he himself had done much to prepare the way for war with Great Britain in 1812, Jefferson was disillusioned by the public debt, high taxation, government spending, flood of paper money, and burgeoning of privileged bank monopolies that accompanied the war.

He had concluded that his beloved Democratic-Republican Party had actually adopted the economic policies of the despised Hamiltonian federalists, and de Tracy's bitter attack on these policies prodded Jefferson to try to get the Traité translated into English. Jefferson gave the new manuscript to Duane again, but the latter went bankrupt, and Jefferson then revised the faulty English translation Duane had commissioned.

Finally, the translation was published as the Treatise on Political Economy, in 1818.[3] Former President John Adams, whose ultra-hard-money and 100 percent-specie-banking views were close to Jefferson's, hailed the de Tracy Treatise as the best book on economics yet published. He particularly lauded de Tracy's chapter on money as advocating "the sentiments that I have entertained all my lifetime." Adams added that:

" banks have done more injury to the religion, morality, tranquility, prosperity, and even wealth of the nation, than they … ever will do good. Our whole banking system, I ever abhorred, I continue to abhor, and shall die abhorring … every bank of discount, every bank by which interest is to be paid or profit of any kind made by the deponent, is downright corruption."

-John Adams

As early as 1790, Thomas Jefferson had hailed Adam Smith's (The Wealth of Nations) as the best book in political economy, along with the work of Turgot. His friend Bishop James Madison (1749–1812), who was president of William & Mary College for 35 years, was the first professor of political economy in the United States. A libertarian who had emphasized early that "we were born free," Bishop Madison had used the Wealth of Nations as his textbook.

de Tracy's Treatise, Thomas Jefferson expressed the "hearty prayer" that the book would become the basic American text in political economy surpassing Smith's The Wealth Of Nations. For a while William & Mary College adopted de Tracy's Treatise under Jefferson's prodding, but this status did not last long. Soon Say's Treatise surpassed de Tracy in the race for popularity in the United States.

THE DIFFERENCE BETWEEN CAPITALISM

& FREE MARKETS

When people discuss the characteristics and possible reforms of capitalism and free markets, they have a tendency to use these two terms interchangeably. In reality the two are quite different things. Let me explain:

Capitalism is defined as a system of ownership of the means of production, specifically the non-labor means of production, which includes factories, tools, equipment, etc. In a capitalistic organization, these means of production are privately owned. Labor is paid a wage for their efforts, and any profits go to the owners of the capital.

A free market system is simply defined as one in which everyone is able to freely sell their goods and services with prices determined by supply and demand.

It is possible to have capitalism without a free market in specific situations. Examples include organizations that have an effective monopoly on a market as we see in the United States today– they can prevent competition from entering the market and can set prices to maximize their own profits instead of being restricted by supply and demand. Another example is the awarding of government no-bid contracts to capitalistic organizations/Corporations.

It is also possible to have a free market that does not involve capitalism. Examples include the traditional farmers market or co-ops competing with each other. In both cases, the clear distinction between owners and workers that is characteristic of capitalism is gone, yet there is still a free market competition that sets prices based on supply and demand.

It's important to keep these distinctions in mind when discussing future economic possibilities.

He (Hamilton) in effect put in to place a system which ultimately has enslaved a entire nation, whereby the average ordinary common citizen, has become the slave of the wealthy/Corporate elite . Whom perceive the common man as no more then a commodity very much like live stock or cattle, with only one purpose. So to produce for their elitist masters capital profit.

So in effect the tragedy of slavery in America not only has it NOT been truly eradicated. But rather with regards to the ever increasing power and hold of the Corporate elite over not only American society but rather also over all other peoples of the world. It is very clear and evident to me that in effect the tragedy of slavery is still very much alive and real today.

So we can conclude that this is still a case of slavery...only this time it doesn't concern a specific race or group of people with in society as it was the case before the American civil war ..but rather this time all of mankind is in threat.

I must make one point abundantly clear. I am a stout and devout supporter of a free laissez-faire economic system, which is void of any influence or control by the state. To be exact I advocate the economical system which was created by the great French economist Destutt de Tracyand, which was in turn also strongly supported by Thomas Jefferson.

However, that being said I would also like to make one point very clear. A point which I have already addressed in my theory " Proletariatism ".

Which is that I do not in any way harbor any animosity towards Capitalists/Corporatists or any other group with in the Commercial sector. My main and only reservation with regards to the mentioned groups. Is ultimatly their involvement or meddling in matters of state.

If Capitalists/Corporatists, can stay out of politics and simply focus their time and energy on what they know best which is the areas of finance and industry,then more power to them. Only as I have also pointed out, The merging of Capitalism with politics and ultimately it replacing the political state with a economical system in its stead or establishing state Capitalism (Socialism) or State Corporatism, is ultimately the inevitable objective of Capitalism.

 So that being the case, regrettably I do not think or believe that Capitalists will ever be able to pull away from politics. After all..their sole objective is to generate monetary or capital profit is it not?..More the better is this not the standard mind set of all those with in the commercial sector?. Thus what better guarantor can a Capitalist possibly have,then being involved in politics and therefore being able to curve legislation which will ultimately help to increase his or her profits or gains??

When I use the term merge when referring to the over stepping of the commercial sector in to the affairs of state. I am in effect referring to the halls of Government being filed with members of the business or Commercial sector, or worst yet, that the political state is in effect replaced with a purely economical one. I would like to elaborate my point here.

The kind of people we need in our government are those whom are statesmen and women, first for most. Individuals whom have never at any point in time either in the past or the present have been involved with or have held any shares, investments or capital interests with in the business or commercial sector. Their sole purpose for entering politics must be with out exception to serve there country period.

They must be statesmen or politicians nothing else, now the reason a individual whom prior to becoming involved with politics was in the business or commercial sector, should not become involved in politics. Is simply because he or she will always be a businessman or woman first and then a politician, and why?. Simply because such individuals have already tasted and have already experienced the luxurious and comfortable life which a successful and lucrative business life can offer.

Therefore such people are tainted with what I call the capital Bug, meaning that no matter what endeavour they undertake no matter what there initial intentions may be even if they are sincere at the start.

Ultimately in the end they will succumb to the itch and fever for acquiring or accumulating wealth, plain and simple there is no way around it. I suppose the proper or correct term for such a state of mind is in fact...GREED.

Warnings against Corporate Capitalism

Thomas Jefferson, was with out question a devout anti Corporatist, whom very early on both saw and understood the very serious threat which this body presented to the future freedoms and liberties of the American people and Americas Republican system. Jefferson wrote the following letter to George Logan in November 1816. Here's the key section with introductory context:

" England exhibits the most remarkable phaenomenon in the universe in the contrast between the profligacy of it's government and the probity of it's citizens. And accordingly it is now exhibiting an example of the truth of the maxim that virtue & interest are inseparable. It ends, as might have been expected, in the ruin of it's people, but this ruin will fall heaviest, as it ought to fall on that hereditary aristocracy which has for generations been preparing the catastrophe. I hope we shall take warning from the example and crush in it's birth the aristocracy of our monied corporations which dare already to challenge our government to a trial of strength and bid defiance to the laws of our country. "

-Thomas Jefferson

In the last year of his life, Jefferson warned of a decadent younger generation of ambitious men who:

"having nothing in them of the feelings or principles of '76, now look to a single and splendid government of an aristocracy, founded on banking institutions, and monied incorporations under the guise and cloak of their favored branches of manufactures, commerce and navigation, riding and ruling over the plundered ploughman and beggared yeomanry."

-Thomas Jefferson

Jefferson, was a relentless critic of the monopolizing of economic power by banks, corporations and those who put their faith in what the third president referred to as "the selfish spirit of commerce (that) knows no country, and feels no passion or principle but that of capital gain.

In the early years of the 19th century, as banks and corporations began to flex their political MUSCLES, he announced that:

"I hope we shall crush… in its birth the aristocracy of our moneyed corporations, which dare already to challenge our government to a trial of strength and bid defiance to the laws of our country."

-Thomas Jefferson

The framers of the American experiment were imperfect men, to be sure. Few were so radical, or so far ahead of their times, as Tom Paine, the wisest of their number. But like Paine, Jefferson was a proud revolutionary against the old order of inherited monarchy, state churches, EMPIRES and the authority of the few over the fate of the many.

Jefferson, as the July 4, 1826 approached, he was invited to appear in Washington for a celebration of the 50th anniversary of the Declaration of Independence. Age and infirmity prevented Jefferson from attending the EVENT. But he sent a message -- his last political statement -- which read:

"May (July 4) be to the world, what I believe it will be -- to some parts sooner, to others later, but finally to all -- the signal of arousing men to burst the chains under which monkish ignorance and superstition had persuaded them to bind themselves, and to assume the blessings and security of self-government. That form (of government) which we have substituted, restores the free right to the unbounded exercise of reason and freedom of opinion. All eyes are opened, or opening, to the rights of man. The general SPREAD of the light of science has already laid open to every view the palpable truth, that the mass of mankind has not been born with saddles on their backs, nor a favored few booted and spurred, ready to ride them legitimately, by the grace of God."

-Thomas Jefferson

Jefferson viewed Banks, with no less suspicion and contempt, after all he was fully aware of the fact that both bodies, the Corporate elite and the Banking elite, weir ultimately the very same, and that together they forwarded

the very same objective. Which was and still is today, so to subjugate and enslave mankind for the sole purpose of capital or monetary profit and gain. He made the following statement regarding Banks, to that effect:

"If the American people ever allow private banks to control the issue of their currency, first by inflation, then by deflation, the banks and corporations that will grow up around them will deprive the people of all property until their children wake up homeless on the continent their Fathers conquered."

-Thomas Jefferson

Very few people are aware that Thomas Jefferson considered freedom from monopolies to be one of the fundamental human rights. But it was very much a part of his thinking during the time when the Bill of Rights was born.

In fact, most Americans at the time never imagined a huge commercial empire sweeping over their land, reminiscent of George R. T. Hewes's "ships of an enormous burthen" with "immense quantities" of goods.

Rather, most of them saw an America made up of people like themselves: farmers.

In fact the very first private corporation to take root in America, between the years of 1801 and 1817 was the second Bank of The United States. The power and influence of this Corporation grew to such level and heights, that by 1830 the bank was one of the largest and most powerful private corporations and, to extend its own power, was even sponsoring its directors and agents as candidates for political office.

A subversive agenda of infiltration of government, a endeavour which has continued right up too today. In fact so much so, that corporate involvement in American politics either directly, in which members of the corporate elite run for public office as candidates.

Or that various Corporations financially back any given candidates campaign, such practices by the Corporates has become so accepted with in the American political system. That many Americans even view it as a crucial and essential part or component of American politics and our free Republican system.

The reality is nothing more further from the truth. This view or perception has been very carefully embedded in to the very subconsciousness of the public. By the corporate elite, so to ultimately enable them in being able to infiltrate the state, and thus be able to use the power of government in forwarding their corporatist agenda and objectives which is the pursuing and accumulating of capital wealth and political power.

 Which in most cases the consequence of such measures were then, and still are today not always in the overall best interest of the country as a whole, but rather they only benefit a small selective portion or fraction of society. The wealthy Corporate elite, the minority at the expense of the ordinary citizen, the common man (The majority).

It is for this reason which I maintain that it is absolutely imperative that the Corporate sector must not ever at any time and in any way what so ever either directly or indirectly be permitted to take part in or to influence government at any level. With regards to candidates whom are from the Corporate/ Commercial sector whom are running for public office I think that it is very important to remember that.

When a statesmen applies him or her self to a task concerning matters of state, he or she dose so with what I call a (Social/Civil Perception) mindset, meaning that they view any given issue or situation on such matters with a mined set which takes in to account and consideration all social and civil aspects or elements with in society.

However, when an individual whom is by profession a businessman or woman, is applied to the same tasks. Their view point or perception regarding society defers greatly. Such individuals whom have devoted most of, or even all of there time to the world of commerce and finance, whereby their only objective and interest has been exclusively the conducting of business and generating of capital profit.

When such individuals are then placed at the helm of government, such perception is in turn implemented in to the political apparatus of any given state as well. In result society is no longer measured based on the elements of civil and social standards or principles but rather is measured in Dollars and Cents.

The human or civil element in such scenarios are void, not taken in to account and are in most cases non existent. Only the profit margin is considered, and this is why a businessman or woman must NOT! ever at any time for any reason be permitted to hold any position within the state.

Thus the halls of government MUST! only be filled with honorable and capable statesmen and women whom have absolutely no ties whatsoever or interests with the Commercial/Business sector. Instead Candidates must be made up of courageous, honorable, patriotic and capable men and women both selected and elected from the ordinary common citizenry.

THE INEVITABLE FATE OF CORPORATE CAPITALISM

By fate I am not suggesting the kind of fate which its outcome is dependent on the course of luck. No, what I am referring to here, is a well planed, Well calculated, pre-designed agenda put in to place so to achieve a specific objective and not a flip of a coin lady luck scenario.

This means that Capitalism/Corporate Capitalism, was in effect designed so to achieve or bring about a single ultimate outcome or objective, Which is state Capitalism (Socialism) or State Corporatism on a global scale, after all Socialism is in effect the largest Corporate body of all.

To those whom still do not grasp the meaning of what I am saying. I must once again maintain that, I am referring to the inevitable outcome of Capitalism/ Corporate Capitalism, and its ultimate objective I am not in any way however referring to an act of God, whereby man has no say or control as to either altering or changing its design.

There is a solution and it is quite simple, the way I see it there are two measures which we must put in to place so to alter the direction which our country is headed. First, we sever all ties either directly or indirectly between the wealthy Corporate elitist and the state.

Capitalists must focus all their efforts to the business of finance and industry, and not matters of state or politics, in the same sense the state (Government) must focus its efforts and energies exclusively with matters of state and politics, and not meddle with or take any active roll in the realm of business and finance.

Secondly We must replace our countries current Hamiltonian Capitalist system with the laissez-faire economic system of Destutt de Tracy which was Jefferson's choice to be adapted for America's economy. Thomas Jefferson translated and edited Destutt de Tracy's work and renamed it " Treatise on Political Economy ".

Yes the definition or the meaning of Socialism is (a concept of the ownership of the means of production without regard to the distribution of produced goods) . However, this definition addresses the mechanics of Socialism and not its core principle or intent. Its as if we say that a rifle or gun is simply a machine which is comprised or made from a number of different parts etc. Which are all then attached together, yes this is correct

However the main purpose and intent for the creation of that rifle is simply to be used as a weapon so to kill. This is the same scenario with Socialism, its main reason for existence is to put in to place a powerful/centralised state, pure and simple.

A state mined you which is not political but rather is a economical one, hence the very definition of Socialism, as described, which is about the state ownership of means of production etc. We can clearly see that it is in fact a purely economical system and not a political one. As for Communism, it is in turn the ultimate goal or agenda of Socialism.

Which is when a universal economical state/system is put in to place (State Capitalism on a global scale) whereby all nations of the world will be governed very much like a plantation. Where all peoples will be perceived as slaves who's only right to life or existence is there monetary worth or value to this system, hence my stance that such a system is in fact economical and not as many have believed to being a political one. After all in Marx's own definition Communism is:

" When all of society, all of economics and all politics are combined into one, perfect, classless, automatic, government-less system based on common ownership of all economic means of production, and social sameness."

I am certain that there are those whom think of me as perhaps being a Leftist or a Marxist, I would like to ask that they do not confuse me with these parasites whom are no better then their fellow Corporate brethren. For the record my entire stance or reservation against the merging of the state with the Commercial sector or vise verse, is based entirely on the moral implications of such a scenario.

Which is as I have said the merging of the Corporate sector with maters of state (Politics). Because ultimately the inevitable out come in such a situation will with out question always be Political corruption. In which case it is always the innocent man and woman on the street (The common man)whom will suffer its consequence.

I would also like to stress as that making profit in business is very well, I have no reservations on this matter. So long of course that this practice remains confined with in the the respective limits and boundaries of the private or Commercial sector and dose not cross over in to politics.

Because once the objective of politics/ state turns to business interests and making capital profit. It is at this moment when innocent human beings suffer and pay the consequences, because In the world of business if a bad business decision is made. Then only the businessman suffers its re-precautions, however, if a business deal falls through which was made by the state.

My response to such an argument is that Yes I agree that we cannot categorise or label all businessmen or women as self serving/greedy/manipulating individuals whom like parasites wish to feed off the sufferings of the people. Of course I do not believe this to be the case.

However, That being said, once an individual from the Commercial sector enters the halls of government, the prospect or possibilities of influencing or cubing legislation so to benefit their business interests and ultimately to increase or improve his or her profit margin will be for the over whelming majority to great of a temptation to resist.

After all, a businessman is a businessman first foremost, and thus he or she will take all measures or will take all necessary steps so to increase their capital profit margins and to forward their business interests. Now if that entails subverting or utilising their position with in the state so to achieve this end then, so be it.

Of course I think that it is also important to note, that in most such cases the individuals whom take such steps honestly do not see their actions to be either morally wrong or bad, after all as I have stated these are businessmen and women whom view all endeavours and ventures through the eyes of a businessman, therefor.

In accordance to business ethics which is basically " This is business not personal " they undertake such tasks with a clear and untroubled conscience simply because they view their actions as simply a normal and standard business practice or approach.

So we can conclude that, even if the intentions of such individuals initially may very well be sincere and well intended, once entering the realm of politics or state. The allure for increasing capital profit and forwarding their business interests is simply to great, and thus they with out meaning to do so, will ultimately in the end succumb to the fever of greed, and greed Is not simply a term to describe ones behaviour or even state of mind. But rather its a spiritual and moral disease.

Its like cancer which embeds it self in to the very subconscious and being of an individual and eats at the very heart and soul of any man or woman which it infects. After all lets not forget that greed is in fact one of the most basic, primitive and darkest instincts and components of human nature.

So then we must ask our selves this single question, should we create an environment whereby enabling this most dangerous and vilest of human natural traits to be able and manifest it self? or should we take all necessary precautions and measures so to confine, restrict and suppress it?.

Therefore, it is for this reason that all necessary measures must be put in to place so that the two worlds of the state and the Commercial sector are never permitted to merge, other wise the inevitable outcome will with out question have dire consequences for the majority of citizens with in society.

CAPITALUTIONISM

OR

EVOLUTIONAL-CAPITALISM

My new theory of Capitalutionism, refers to the four inevitable, Evolutional stages of Capitalism/Corporate Capitalism. This process is categorised in to four consecutive levels or stages:

(National Level)

1- Economic Capitalism: All focus and activity is exclusively involved with matters of Finance   and Industry.

2- Crony or Corporate Capitalism: This refers to a process whereby Capitalism spills over in to politics and via various special interest or lobby groups it is able to influence government legislation and policies etc.

3- State Capitalism or Socialism (State Corporatism): This refers to when Capitalism ultimately replaces the conventional national government or state and essentially becomes the state or system of government.

(International Level)

4- The final and ultimate stage, with in the Evolutional path of Capitalism is when State Capitalism (Socialism) or (State Corporatism), is spread across the glob as a ruling power. This is the point in time when the system has been installed in every country of the world.

When this occurs, all traditional or conventional systems of governments and politics will be cast aside and in its stead a single universal global system is put in to place, a New Universal System.

This system is not based on any single or given political doctrine or ideology, but rather it is a purely Corporate Capitalist system, an economical system whereby all peoples of the world are no longer perceived as citizens, but rather they are viewed as commodities very much like live stock, cattle or sheep.

Where before every person had the natural right to life as a human being, under the new system this is no longer the case. Instead a persons right to life is measured exclusively on the bases of his or her economical or monetary worth or value to the system. This final stage on an international level is when we have pure universal State Corporatism or Communism.

FREE BANKING

LESSER OF THE TWO EVILS

As it is that unfortunately for over two centuries the world especially the United states has been infected with the disses of Hamilton's Corporate Capitalism, and in result of his poison we have also become subjugated and enslaved by the world banking Corporate elite.

and therefore are unable to pull our selves out from under this mammoth mountain granite of greed, I suggest that if we cannot rid our selves from the fever of Banks then we should at least attempt at choosing a system which is of the lesser evil. What I am purposing is to adapt the Banking system which is the most incorruptible and the least influenced by the state and the Corprate elites. This is the " Free Banking System ".

FREE BANKING

Free banking refers to a monetary arrangement in which banks are subject to no special regulations beyond those applicable to most enterprises, and in which they also are free to issue their own paper currency (banknotes).

In a free banking system, market forces control the supply of total quantity of banknotes and deposits that can be supported by any given stock of cash reserves, where such reserves consist either of a scarce commodity (such as gold) or of an artificially limited stock of "fiat" money issued by a central bank.

In the strictest versions of free banking, however, there either is no role at all for a central bank, or the supply of central bank money is supposed to be permanently "frozen." There is, therefore, no agency capable of serving as a "lender of last resort" in the usually understood sense of the term.

Nor is there any government insurance of banknotes or bank deposit accounts. Supporters include Fred Foldvary, David D. Friedman, Friedrich Hayek, George Selgin, Lawrence H. White. Steven Horwitz, and Richard Timberlake.

The free banking movement got its modern start in 1977 with The Denationalization of Money, by economist Friedrich Hayek, who advocated that national governments stop claiming a monopoly on the issuing of currency, and allow private issuers like banks to voluntarily compete to do so.

According to Hayek, instead of a national government issuing a specific currency, use of which is imposed on all members of its economy by force in the form of legal tender laws, private businesses should be allowed to issue their own forms of money, deciding how to do so on their own.

Hayek advocates a system of private currency in which financial institutions create currencies that compete for acceptance. Stability in value is presumed be the decisive factor for acceptance. Hayek makes the assumption that competition will favor currencies with the greatest stability in value since a devalued currency hurts creditors, and an upward-revalued currency hurts debtors.

Hence users would choose the moneys which they expected to offer a mutually acceptable intersection between depreciation and appreciation. Hayek suggests that institutions may find through experimentation that an extensive basket of commodities forms the ideal monetary base. Institutions would issue and regulate their currency primarily through loan-making, and secondarily through currency buying and selling activities.

It is postulated that the financial press would report daily information on whether institutions are managing their currencies within a previously-defined tolerance. Hayek's effort has been cited by economists George Selgin, Richard Timberlake, and Lawrence White.

As I have pointed out the most important issue here is to prevent any single group rather it be a private entity or the state from gaining any real and complete control over the economy and capital.

so, as I have said I think our best choice would be to adapt the Free Banking system this way neither the state or any other single body would be able to monopolise the currency and consequently will not be able to claim total control over the economy and capital.

HOW CAN WE TAKE BACK AMERICA?

I would like to take this moment and reflect upon a few issues which I consider to be absolutely imperative that need to be addressed, if we wish to ever return our country back to her former self.
First, we must eliminate the hold which the wealthy Corporate elite have over our society by depriving them of their source of power, which I have broken down in to two components or parts, They are as follows:

1- We must as I have explained before, once and for all sever all there their influence both directly and indirectly with our countries politics.This is what I call eliminating there Executive Arm, which is there ability via special interest or lobby groups to influence legislation and therefore being able to push forward political measures which will ultimately be to there and (NOT!) the collective interest of the American people.

Of course the eliminating the ability of the elitist Capitalists from being able to influence legislation by severing the influence of there agents (Special interest groups/Lobbyists is only effective if the two bodies (The state and Corporate Capitalists) remain as two separate bodies and entities.

However, once Capitalism or Corporate Capitalism merges with politics, whereby the conventional state or system of government, is cast aside and corporate Capitalism, in effect becomes the state or government (Socialism) or State Capitalism/ State Corporatism.

Severing the influence of spacial interest or lobby groups with matters of the state is no longer a viable or effective measure to be taken, for as I have explained. At this stage or level, the Corporates them selves essentially have become the state or government. intact and unchanged.

When this happens there is only one option left available, that is to replace all members of both the House Of Representatives and the Senate, with newly elected Representatives, Candidates whom are both selected and elected from the ordinary common citizen body.

I refer to this process as (Political Martial Law), whereby all government agencies are cleansed from the ajentors or agents of the elitist Capitalists and in turn there positions are filed with honorable and capable states men and women, chosen from the common citizenry.

Who's only interest is not the pursuing of there own financial and political carriers but rather, to serve there country and to strive for the collective interest and good of there fellow countrymen and there country.

2- Secondly we must then focus on eliminating the hold and influence which the elitists have over the social structure of our society. I refer to this as there Legislative Arm, meaning there ability to influence and manipulate the mind set and psyche of the American people. Whereby the populace are subverted indoctrinated or subvertly desensitised, so to think and behave in a specific pre-determined manor, which will ultimately bring the people under there total and complete control.

So to be cultivated or used for the sole purpose of generating monetary profit and political gain for there elitist masters. Now just how is such a scenario achieved?...Basically by altering the view point of society as to what is most important in our lives.

Which is undermining and devaluing the importance of morality, and ethical values whereby they are categorised as minor issues and are given a back seat, to the presence and importance of worldly positions and wealth.

The reasoning for this is very simple, by implementing such view points in to the minds and subconsciousness of the populace.

Whereby the people are overcome with the fever and desire for the pursuit of worldly positions and wealth they become susceptive to becoming infected with the daises or ailment of greed. Where there only interest in life becomes a continuous and relentless desire and pursuit for the quest and the accumulating of wealth, worldly positions and pleasures.

This in turn generates corruption in all areas of society, most importantly in the halls of government. In such a scenario where the principles of morality, ethical values and even loyalty and devotion to ones country are compromised, laxed and are viewed as irrelevant and insignificant in comparison with the importance of gaining wealth and power.

naturally those whom control societies wealth (The wealthy elitists) are then able to utilize there vast wealth and by taking advantage of the immoral and unethical mined set embedded in society, They are through bribery and payoffs able to gain a footing in to government, and in time ultimatly controle or even become the state.

In order to revers this process and to reclaim our country, also to place America, back on the correct path which had been intended by our founders, we must put in to effect the following measures:

1-Implement my new theory "Proletariatism " in to the political apparatus of the United States. Now as to how this can be achieved?. The process though may be to some degree extensive and may entail a lengthily process, it is never the less very simple to execute or carry out. Basically the process must begin at the state levels, with the electing of candidates for Congress.

Whereby the residents of their respective states must only cast there support and vote for those candidates whom are statesmen and women of humble backgrounds and are members of the common ordinary citizen body, whom have no ties, investments or interests in any area of the Commercial or business sector...PERIOD.

It is of absolute importance that this point is especially adhered to with out exception, for reasons I have already addressed. Once we are able to fill the halls of Congress with such candidates, then it would not be difficult so to push forward the Proletariatism initiative.

By implementing Preoletariatism in to the political structure of America, we achieve the following two objectives:

a. The first is political, whereby the power and control of government or the state is taken away from the wealthy Corporate elite, the (Minority) and is returned back to the common ordinary people the (Majority).

b. The second objective is as I have pointed out economical. Whereby severing or eliminating the ability of the elitists in being able to monopolise there political hold over the countries government, and thus enabling their ability to manipulate and push forward legislation which is put forth not in the best interest of the collective citizen body.

But rather instead for the sole purpose of generating monetary and political gain and profit specifically for them selves the wealthy elite. Therefore by returning the control of state back to the citizens, whereby all members of government are in effect both selected and elected from the common citizen body (The majority) and not the wealthy elite (The minority).

whom in turn will be in the position so to push forward legislation which will ultimately bring about economical prosperity for the collective good of the entire populace, instead of only serving the interest of a minute and small portion of the citizenry (The wealthy elite).

2- The second measure, is to once and for all replace Alexander Hamilton's, economical policy of corporate welfare, protectionist tariffs, central banking, and a large public debt, with De-Tracy's Laissez-faire free economic system, which was very much supported by Thomas Jefferson.

Hamilton's system advocates what is termed as "The commercial state" concept (and its important variant, commercial society) which is sometimes also associated with Adam Ferguson's concept of civil society and refers to a government or political state devoted primarily to the promotion and advancement of commercial interests.

It is this concept " The Commercial State " which Hamilton's system advocates which is the root or cause of the large centralised and corrupt government that exists in America today. As I have stressed many times before, the merging of the state with the commercial sector must be avoided at all costs, a scenario which Hamilton's system strongly promotes and advocates.

The reasoning for this is simple, this is because the merging of politics with the commercial sector (Corporate Capitalism) will ultimately lead to the replacing of the political state with a economical system in its stead or establishing state Capitalism (Socialism) or State Corporatism.

So therefore we must conclude, that the permanent removal of Hamilton's system, which essentially is the bridge whereby the two sectors the Commercial sector and the state are able to merge, is paramount and essential if we are ever to cleanse our government of corruption, and return it back to the people. And replacing it with a truly free market system or a laissez-faire economy.

The very type of economecal policy which Thomas Jefferson had origenally intended to implament in America. The system which Jefferson advocated was a system created by Destutt de Tracy, and explained in his book " A Treatise on Political Economy " which had been both edited and translated by Jefferson himself.

Many Americans, today are overwhelmed with a sense of fear, uncertainty and despair with regards to the many radical changes which have been taking shape in America, especially over these last few years. Whereby our freedoms, Liberties, our way of life and even our right to practice our Christian faith has been challenged, undermined and scrutinised.

Many Americans, are perhaps for the first time in there lives faced with a scenario which is totally alien to any thing they have ever experienced before. Many ask and wonder..." What is there to be done?"...." How can we turn back the tide and cast aside this black cloud which has engulfed our country? ".

In search for answers in consequence many Americans, are looking to the various Conservative groups, candidates and elected officials for answers and help.

In short they look to the system for guidance still believing that the political apparatus in our country is still divided between good and bad, and that there still remains a positive element with in American politics that holds true to the principles and ideals of freedom and liberty, or adheres to the laws set forth in the our countries sacred document the United states Constitution.

However this point of view or perception is by far in my view any thing but the truth. Fact of the matter is that our countries entire political system with out exception is and has been for some time in effect seized to being the system of old, the system which our founding fathers had established or what they had intended for America.

Many of us Americans, seem to be oblivious to the fact that our political system as it stands today no longer harbors any positive elements nor is it comprised of two separate entities of good and evil.

But rather it has in fact become a single united apparatus forwarding not the laws of our Constitution nor the principles of freedom and Liberty but rather a single objective in enslaving the people for the sole purpose of generating both financial and political gain for the minority wealthy elite.

Now many ask " if we can no longer be dependent or place our trust upon our political system rather it be the right or left then what is the solution?". Before I answer that question, I would first like to take this moment and address one very important issue which I feel I must address to my fellow countrymen and women.

That is the matter concerning a armed rebellion or uprising by the people against the state. I cannot stress enough that such a view or mined set is in every way purely madness and ludicrous, please allow me to elaborate.

Many Americans, feel that the only way of reclaiming there freedoms and liberties and taking back there country from a ever growing powerful state is to emulate the actions of our founding fathers during our glorious war of independence back in 1776. Though I hold this view to be truly courageous and noble in principle.

Proletaritaism, is in fact not a political movement, doctrine, ideology or party. It is a proactive political principle, element and ideological tool which can be easily adapted and implemented into a pre-existing system of any free state, be it a Democracy or a Republic. When a Democracy or a Republic utilizes Proletariatism, all pre-existing Constitutional laws and principles remain in place, intact and unchanged.

However in reality as I have said such a view is pure madness, and why?, because of one major factor...WEAPONRY...the weapons used back in 1776 are a far cry to today's modern weapons, whereby the the Colonial farmers weir in most cases equipped with the very same type of fire arm and weaponry which the British regular forces weir equipped with.

When Proletariatism, is adapted only those citizens who are of the Proletariat, the common working class citizenry, which includes but is not limited to farmers, factory workers, welders, builders, plumbers, electricians, small business owners, professors, school teachers and so on, are allowed to hold any political office.

there was no real difference or distinction between the two, however unlike then today the state has access to an army which is equipped with every conceivable modern weapon known to man, in many cases some which your ordinary citizen has not even heard of.

I mean for a ordinary citizen to take up arms against a well fortified, well equipped, well trained and well supplied state, as our founding fathers had done in 1776 is like using the same kind of Black powder rifle and tactics in a modern/mechanised/High technical war. It doesn't take a genius to ascertain as to what the outcome in such a scenario would be.

So my advise to my fellow countrymen is that we must totally put out of our minds any such endeavour, and instead focus our efforts on attempting to restore our beloved country by all legal and peaceful means, by utilising the meassures which I have laied out.

COMMON CORE A CORPORATE OBJECTIVE

Many in America, view the Common Core educational system or curriculum to be the work of scholars and political statesmen. However this perception is any thing but the truth. In fact it is a purely business motivated objective set forth by the Corporate elite, for the sole purpose of creating a world filled not with independent minded, intelligent and rational people, but rather to create a world filed with economical workers and slaves for the specific purpose of working and generating capital profit.

Now as I have said many will dispute this fact and will adamantly proclaim that the Common Core agenda is in fact a political and scholarly objective one and not a Corporatist one. So I think that it is important for us to take a closer look in to this system and see just whom weir its creators and whom in fact financed its conception.

The key architect and developer of Common Core was not as many believe to be a scholar or politician but rather instead it was a businessman by the name of David Coleman, and his system is a system which was designed by a Corporatists forwarding a global Corporatist agenda and objective. In 2009, the NGA convened a group of people to work on developing the standards for Educational reform or Common Core (CC) .

This team included David Coleman, William McCallum of the University of Arizona, Phil Daro, and Student Achievement Partners founders Jason Zimba, and Susan Pimentel to write standards in the areas of mathematics and literacy.

Proletaritaism, is in fact not a political movement, doctrine, ideology or party. It is a proactive political principle, element and ideological tool which can be easily adapted and implemented into a pre-existing system of any free state, be it a Democracy or a Republic. When a Democracy or a

Republic utilizes Proletariatism, all pre-existing
Constitutional laws and principles remain in place, intact and
unchanged.

There are only two main modifications made to present systems with the
adapting of Proletariatism, one is who will be allowed to run as a
candidate and hold office, the other deals with funding. In the first case,
dealing with who are allowed to run as a candidate and hold office, a
change is made as to which group, class or citizen body are permitted to
hold or run for public office as active elected participants in there
countries politics and government .

When Proletariatism, is adapted only those citizens who are of the
Proletariat, the common working class citizenry, which includes but is
not limited to farmers, factory workers, welders, builders, plumbers,
electricians, small business owners, professors, school teachers and
so on, are allowed to hold any political office.

Only members from this group of citizens are permitted to run for public office to thus
become active members of there countries politics. Whereby citizens who belong to the
wealthy, elitist groups, or upper class, the minority Capitalists, consisting of Industrialists,
Bankers, large manufacturers, Corporations, etc. are prohibited from ever running for or
holding public office at any level.

Proletaritaism, is in fact not a political movement, doctrine,
ideology or party. It is a proactive political principle, element
and ideological tool which can be easily adapted and
implemented into a pre-existing system of any free state, be
it a Democracy or a Republic. When a Democracy or a
Republic utilizes Proletariatism, all pre-existing
Constitutional laws and principles remain in place, intact and
unchanged.

There are only two main modifications made to present systems with the
adapting of Proletariatism, one is who will be allowed to run as a
candidate and hold office, the other deals with funding. In the first case,
dealing with who are allowed to run as a candidate and hold office, a
change is made as to which group, class or citizen body are permitted to
hold or run for public office as active elected participants in there
countries politics and government .

When Proletariatism, is adapted only those citizens who are of the
Proletariat, the common working class citizenry, which includes but is
not limited to farmers, factory workers, welders, builders, plumbers,
electricians, small business owners, professors, school teachers and
so on, are allowed to hold any political office.

Only members from this group of citizens are permitted to run for public office to thus become active members of there countries politics. Whereby citizens who belong to the wealthy, elitist groups, or upper class, the minority Capitalists, consisting of Industrialists, Bankers, large manufacturers, Corporations, etc. are prohibited from ever running for or holding public office at any level.

Now Coleman was a Consultant with the Global Corporate conglomerate McKinsey & Co. Whic is a global business/Corporate consultant firm which has direct links with many major Corporations across glob. They are not a law firm. But rather their speciality is to offers services in how companies and corporations can better operate their Corporations etc.

Another very interesting piece of information regarding whom all in fact weir and still are behind the Common Core agenda or objective. Which clearly substantiates the argument to the effect that it is in every way a globalist/Corporate objective, which has been able via their many influences and footings in to the halls of our government to influence legislation and thus push forward this unholy objective

many major Corporations have invested colossal amounts of capital in to the Common Core objective. The federal government is acquiring a massive amount of data that can be sold to the highest bidders," says Carole Hornsby Haynes, Ph.D., a curriculum specialist and writer. "This is an invasion of student and family privacy and a violation of our 4th Amendment rights. The education-technology buzzards are circling overhead and, having smelled the strong scent of money, are salivating at the thought of making billions from this new goldmine.

The two most important groups in this multi billion dollar game are with out question Bill Gates and a number of Rockefeller affiliated companies and Corporatist groups. Please refer to the following documents and information to this effect:

Gates Money and Common Core
The following post is a series detailing Bill Gates' mammoth purchasing of the Common Core State Standards (CCSS). The organizations includ a comprehensive listing of the $173.5 million in Gates funding designated for CCSS as of October 4, 2013. All organizations receiving

Gates CCSS funding can be found here, with the exception of one grant to the Fordham Foundation, which can be found here.

The list copied below can be found in Word document form here: Gates Money for CCSS to Businesses and Nonprofits. Gates CCSS Funding to Businesses and (As of Yet Unexamined) Nonprofits Bill Gates has paid a total of $51.5 million to the businesses and nonprofits on the list below. Most of these recipients agree to the simple directive of "implementing the Common Core State Standards":

Achievement Network $3,452,501
America's Promise $500,000
Battelle for Kids $249,808
Benchmark Education Company, LLC $25,000
BetterLesson, Inc. $3,527,240
Center for Applied Linguistics $249,396
Center for Curriculum Redesign, Inc. $198,000
Center for Teaching Quality, Inc. $645,307

Common Core, Inc. $550,844
Common Ground Software, Inc. $500,000
ConnectEDU, Inc. $499,375
Council for a Strong America $1,550,000
Creative Commons Corporation $1,099,687
Cristo Rey Network $556,006
Education Development Center, Inc. $211,795
Expeditionary Learning Outward Bound, Inc. $250,000
Filament Games, LLC $25,000
Fund for Public Schools, Inc. $1,815,810

JUMP Math $698,587
iCivics, Inc. $500,000
Khan Academy, Inc. $5,544,028
Learning Forward $999,795
LearnZillion, Inc. $1,215,525
Massachusetts Business Alliance for Education, Inc. $151,431
MetaMetrics, Inc. $3,468,005
National Center for Family Literacy, Inc. $236,796

National Math and Science Initiative, Inc. $248,760
National Paideia Center $659,788
New Teacher Center $250,000

New Venture Fund $578,000
New Visions for Public Schools, Inc. $8,399,935
Pennsylvania Partnerships for Children $240,000
Prichard Committee for Academic Excellence $198,206
Reasoning Mind, Inc. $742,996

Research in Action, Inc. $1,309,409
Rockefeller Philanthropy Advisors, Inc. $4,618,652
Scholastic, Inc. $4,463,541
Six Red Marbles, LLC $500,000
State Education Technology $500,000
WestEd $30,000

The post above are the larger Gates payouts.

BetterLesson, Inc. BetterLesson, Inc. Proponents of CCSS are fond of repeating that CCSS is "not a curriculum." However, Gates, who desperately wishes to "implement" CCSS, is willing to pay for that curriculum in the name of "helping teachers transition" and "students master":

> BetterLesson, Inc. Date: October 2012
> Purpose: to support the development of courses, aligned to the Common Core State Standards, for the purposes of helping teacher's transition to common core and increasing their students' ability to master the content Amount: $3,527,240 [Purpose emphasis added.]
>
> The founder of BetterLesson, Alex Grodd, is a Teach for America (TFA) alum. So, here we have Gates paying a teaching temp to write CCSS lessons for those who view teaching as a career. No one need guess what "student mastery" means to a former TFAer. Score well on that be-all-end-all standardized test.

Let's try another one. Achievement Network
Achievement Network has a signature reform board of directors, including hedge fund managers and education business "founders." Achievement Network received two CCSS Gates grants, the larger of which is detailed below:
Achievement Network.

 Date: November 2012 Purpose: to support implementation of the Common Core State Standards by building the capacity of school leaders and teachers to address the instructional shifts through interim assessments, coaching, network collaboration, and access to resources Amount: $3,002,252 Thus, Gates has paid an organization run by non-educators to aid educators in implementing CCSS. Sensible, isn't it?

Rockefeller Philanthropy Advisors, Inc.
How about Rockefeller Philanthropy Advisors? Yet another organization with a board of directors heavy on hedge fund managers and business owners. And what is their CCSS task from Gates?
It's a terrible sentence. (Bolded below).

Rockefeller Philanthropy Advisors, Inc. Date: October 2011
Purpose: to partner with other foundations to support a project fund supporting state-led efforts aligning
higher education placement requirements with college readiness assessments developed through the
Common Core assessment consortia Amount: $4,618,652 [Purpose emphasis added.]

Translation: Rockefeller Philanthropy is to join with other organizations in helping states to take the higher ed entrance requirements and make them fit with the CCSS assessments. Rockefeller and other groups are going to help the states to be "state-led."

New Visions for Public Schools, Inc. Moving on to New Visions for Public Schools. In New York City, the public schools now "shop" for a bureaucracy to which to report in place of a district superintendent. New Visions for Public Schools is one such bureaucracy. These organizations now directing the public schools are euphemistically called school support organizations.New Visions for New Schools is very CCSS friendly. Below are the details on the larger of the two Gates CCSS grants it received:

New Visions for Public Schools, Inc. Date: November 2010
Purpose: to support the Common Core/Career and College initiative (C4) effort designed to improve student achievement and
teacher effectiveness through key strategies
Amount: $8,149,935

Gates paid New Visions for Public Schools to "improve student achievement" which, of course, means maxing those standardized test scores. Perhaps Gates should have paid NYC Mayor Bloomberg to have his minions reasonably set the cutoff scores of New York's first CCSS assessment so as to not fail most of the students. It might have cost Bill some eight-figure dough since Bloomberg

is apparently proud of his accomplishment. One more: Khan Academy.
Khan Academy Khan Academy's "team" includes a number of
individuals formerly with McKinsey and Company, the consulting firm
formerly employing CCSS "architect" David Coleman. McKinsey's
interest is in gathering data. McKinsey is in deep with CCSS. Consider
this excerpt by Mona McDermott of United Opt Out:

...McKinsey and Co., which is a global consulting firm. Their big thing is called "Big
Data."... They believe that the data is the answer to all things right now, (and) as you can
see they've got their fingerprints all over everything in the Common Core. For one thing,
David Coleman was one of the architects of the Common Core. He created the Student
Achievement Partners, which helped develop standards, (and he) was a former
consultant for McKinsey.

Lou Gerstner, who is the co-founder of Achieve, was the
former director at McKinsey & Co., and Sir Michael Barber
was a former consultant McKinsey (and) is now one of the
CEOs at Pearson. Pearson partners with the PARCC
Consortium for the assessments. I wrote about Coleman,
Student Achievement Partners, and Achieve in my first post
of this series.

Gates generously funded both Student Achievement Partners and
Achieve for this CCSS propagation. And here we have him funding
Khan Academy- a foothold of McKinsey and Company:
Khan Academy Date: October 2010 Purpose: to provide general
operating support, expanding Khan Academy's leadership and staff
capacity to map Khan Academy

content to the Common Core high school standards, improve
assessments, and enhance the user interface Amount: $1,464,667
Date: July 2011 Purpose: to develop the remaining K-12 math
exercises to ensure full coverage of the Common Core math standards
and form

a small team to implement a blended learning model Amount: $4,079,361 Gates is
paying Khan Academy to create CCSS curriculum. To do so, Khan Academy needed to
expand its staff. So, Gates paid for that. Its team now includes 47 (mostly young) people,
6 of whom are formerly of McKinsey.

fashion, many of the young people held titles from their former employment meant to impress: vice president, lead designer, program manager, business manager, director. Only one out of 47 mentions a substantive career (15 years) in classroom teaching.

Gates: Spending Billions But Just "Not Sure" Bill Gates has already spent billions on education reform. (I was tempted to write "countless billions," but that is not true. One is able to tabulate an up-to-date grand total using the Gates grants search engine. I invite anyone ambitious enough to take on
this task

Special Interest Groups Continue
to Dominate the Reigns

You'd think federal standards would be developed by the federal government, right? Not in this case. Instead, big business and special interest groups created Common Core State Standards. You see, in the mid-90s the National Governors Association, along with several national corporations, created Achieve, Inc.

a D.C.-based non-profit that's the "leading voice for the college-and career-ready agenda." Achieve financial contributors include big businesses like AT&T (T), The Boeing Company (BA), Chevron (CVX), Cisco (CSCO), IBM(IMB) and Prudential (PRU).

Proletaritaism, is in fact not a political movement, doctrine, ideology or party. It is a proactive political principle, element and ideological tool which can be easily adapted and implemented into a pre-existing system of any free state, be it a Democracy or a Republic. When a Democracy or a Republic utilizes Proletariatism, all pre-existing Constitutional laws and principles remain in place, intact and unchanged.

Achieve began developing federal benchmarks and standards in 1998 and soon after, sponsored a summit to determine the "must have skills" desired by America's top employers. Put simply: the Common Core initiative was started and continues to be pushed by politicians and special interest groups – not educators or parents.

A HISTORY of Grooming the System

In 2007, the Bill and Melinda Gates Foundation and the Eli Broad Foundation partnered and pledged $60 million to create what's now known as Common Core. The following year, the Gates Foundation gave over $2 million to politicians and other investors to promote the adoption of a federal curriculum. But it gets even more muddied in big business.

In 2009, executives from the Gates Foundation were hired as Secretary of Education Arne Duncan's Chief of Staff and as the head of the Office of Innovation and Improvement. Since joining the initiative, the Gates Foundation has invested more than $160 million in the Common Core State Standards.

But the Gates Foundation and the Eli Broad Foundation aren't alone. The GE Foundation, of General Electric (GE), and its CEO Jeffrey Immelt, have made investments of their own. That's right, the very same Immelt who said of China: "State-run communism may not be your cup of tea, but their government works.

You know?" And this mess of a web only gets bigger with key players such as the Department of Education, Secretary of Education Duncan, Achieve Inc. and Pearson Publishing (PSO) all pushing the standards onto teachers and students.

And don't forget the mouthpieces like the Fordham Institute, Hunt Institute and Jeb Bush's The Foundation for Excellence in Education, who all use their platforms to push the Common Core agenda.

Blatant Ulterior Motives

The education system is just another CASH cow to heave around for these industry giants (not that they're the only ones using our education system for self-gain). Pearson Publishing stands to gain a lot from Common Core. The UK-based company operates in more than 70 countries but 60% of its sales come from North America.

Pearson already has a monopoly on public education in America and only stands to gain from Common Core implementation. According to Peter Cohen, CEO of Pearson's K-12 division, Pearson School, "It's a really big deal.

The Common Core standards are affecting literally every part of the business we're involved in." I'm sure it does when Common Core is estimated to cost districts nearly $8 billion in educational materials just to implement the standards.

Don't get me wrong: Standards in education aren't necessarily a bad thing. To be sure, they aid in holding students and teachers accountable, and they often influence successes in education. However, the problem stems from who is creating these standards, and those who should be but aren't – states, educators and parents, for example, have no part in developing the standards.

Maybe Common Core's creators and investors had good intentions in developing the benchmarks, but we all know that the road to hell is paved with good intentions. Somewhere along the way, any good intentions that existed have long been trampled by the pursuit of money holding public office at any level.

"Nobody stops to ask what education is for, because the answer is implicitly accepted by all: an education is for getting a job. It is, in other words, for being a cog in the giant machine of post-industrial capitalism."

"We are not speaking of education in the narrower sense, but of that other education in virtue from youth upwards, which makes a man eagerly pursue the ideal perfection of citizenship, and teaches him how rightly to rule and how to obey. This is the only education which, upon our view, deserves the name; that other sort of training, which aims at the acquisition of wealth or bodily strength, or mere cleverness apart from intelligence and justice, is mean and illiberal, and is not worthy to be called education at all." -- Plato, Laws I, 643e

The Untold History of Modern Education in the U.S., explores how men of great wealth in the early 1900s introduced compulsory education and conspired to manipulate all facets of public education through Non-Government Foundations to create an object-based education system.

Through their well-funded NGOs, the Rockefellers, Guggenheims, Vanderbilts, Morgans, and Fords were able to create, by design, a manageable work labor force that would not challenge the status quo thus making people more predictable and easier to control.

" We are creating the most meaningful reform of school education in a generation designed to fundamentally transform America's education system. "

-- *President Barrack Obama*

Today these same large institutions are still very much in power and control greatly influencing our public education system. They have been joined by the mega Bill and Melinda Gates Foundation (Microsoft) as well the Joyce Foundation (timber), Walton Foundation (Walmart) and Broad Foundation (Kaufman/Broad Homebuilders) helping to create and implement a one-size-fits-all, global IT-based education system.

In January 2002, President Bush signed the "No Child Left Behind Act" (NCLB) into law which tied school funding to a punish/reward test performance system. President Bush's message at that time was, "Test all students every year to hold schools accountable for closing achievement gaps.

Just after taking office in 2009, President Obama announced his "Race To The Top" (RTTT) program, rewarding critical school funding to only those schools who showed excellent improvement in test performance.

He dangled $ 4.3 Billion to reward schools 'points' for satisfying certain federally determined performance-based standards. There was another added kicker though. The funding would only be allocated to those states and school districts who "voluntarily" subscribed to the newly created Common Core States Initiative (CCSI) program.

In June 2008, the Bill and Melinda Gates Foundation granted $2.2 million to the Hunt Institute for Educational Leadership to promote the adoption of national academic standards and host a conference with the National Governors Association (NGA) to explore strategies to make the United States a "global leader in education".

The NGA along with the Council of Chief State School Officials (CCSSO), NGO's based out of Washington D.C., began accepting grants from private organizations to write Common Core guidelines.

Common Core is described by proponents as a utopian education for the 21st century with primary, almost exclusive, emphasis from grades K-12 on mathematics and English language arts through "disruptive innovation" using the latest in "educational technological advancements".

In reality, as you will read below, it is a critical step towards the stated goals of the wealthy elite to uniformly 'mono-mind' the global educational system, create a 24/7/365 community at our public schools, and to develop a "from-cradle-to-work-force-ready" individual.

The real big picture goals for the reformation of our public schools comes directly from Arne Duncan, the U.S. Secretary of Education. These excerpts are direct quotes from his interview on the Charlie Rose Show in March of 2009:

-"I think our schools should be open 12, 13 hours a day and open 6 to 7 days per week."
-"Attach HEALTH CARE clinics to the development of our schools."
-"Schools become the center of our community life so great things can happen."
-"We can bring in NGO's to help with the schools….and turn the schools over to these NGO's after 3 p.m. until 9 p.m."

-"Work collectively and collaboratively with private institutions to provide this vast array of educational enrichment social and even MEDICAL services to the families…to meet the students' social and emotional needs."
-"Today, you have single parents working, parents working 2-3 jobs, children going home to no-parent families and our schools have not kept up. And I think this is an opportunity to create what a 21st century school has to look like. This needs to be the norm not the exception and all of our stores need to be open longer." (italicized emphasis added to apparent "slip" of the tongue)
-"This BATTLE is more than just about education, this battle is about social justice."

Private/Public Partnerships (PPP) are the legal vehicles being used to implement Mr. Duncan's plans for schools being the central hub of our communities with big business partnership.

 PPP involves a contract between a public sector authority and a private party, in which the private party provides a public service or project and gains financial, technical and operational benefits while government takes the liability and the risk in the project while the NGO's write educational policies to be enacted in the schools.

These NGO's, like the Gates Foundation, help drive the national and global academic curriculum, standards and performance criterion that schools must adhere to or risk reduced school funding from federal and state levels. Local school districts are virtually excluded from this process.

The National Governors Association and the CCSSO created the Common Core Standards Initiative (CCSI). Legally, they also retain "all right, title, and interest to the same" meaning they own the Common Core curriculum copyrights and use is granted by a Public License from them.

This means that no one, including teachers, administrators or parents, can alter the contents of the CC curriculum without facing possible legal action. Additionally, states cannot amend the Common Core States Initiative due to the "living work" statement in the terms and agreement clauses.

The NGA and CCSSO are private corporations based in Washington D.C. and though many of the members of NGA are our countries state governors, while they are in Washington D.C. conducting business for NGA or CCSSO, they are acting solely as lobbyists because Washington D.C. is a "District" not a state.

This allows the governors to conduct business for their lobbying association while in the District of Columbia and then, when they return to the states, they don once more their governor hats to mandate the CC agenda agreed upon by the NGA and CCSSO associations. And it is all perfectly legal.

NGA and CCSSO members meet in a specific building in Washington D.C. called the "Hall of States" owned by the State Service Organization (SSO). The Hall of States acts as caretaker for many NGO incorporated associations effectively acting as a government inside a government.

According to the Council of Chief State School Officials website, they are a non-partisan, non-profit organization comprised of public officials partnering with a vast array of NGOs, including lobbyist groups like Software and Information Industry Association (SIIA).

SIIA serve and represent more than 150 member for-profit companies providing software, digital content and other technologies for public and private schools including Microsoft, Apple, Wireless Generation, IBM and Discovery Education – a spin-off of the television channel that gave us Amish Mafia.

Also in affiliation with CCSSO are some of the biggest publishing houses: McGraw-Hill, Scholastic, and Pearson who produce the data and educational material provided to public schools. Together, these technology, media and publishing corporations work with policymakers to integrate their products into curricula.

Since its inception in 2008, the creation of Common Core has largely been funded by the richest man in the word, Bill Gates. From 2009 to 2011 alone, he has donated over $22 million to CCSSO and $2,259,780 to the National Governors Association.

When Common Core was debated at the Indiana State Capitol, who showed up to advocate for Common Core? "Stand for Children", which Bill Gates funds. He also funds the League of Education Voters, the Center for Reinventing Public Education and the Partnership for Learning, all Common Core advocates; Mr. Gates also owns Editorial Projects in Education, parent of Education Week magazine.

The Common Core system, is no more then a specially tailored and designed state Curriculum, designed so to subvertly indoctrinate or Desensitize students. The objective is not so much but dose include the altering, changing or miss presenting of information.

But rather it is a system specially designed so to alter the viewpoint of students in how they perceive, interpret or understand any given political, social or religious issue or situation. The exact model of this state sponsored system under different or variant names has and still is used in countries such as Iran, China, Cuba, Venezuela, North Korea and the former Soviet Union.

The root and core of this system was in fact first developed in 1810 by Johann Gottlieb Fichte, who was the head of philosophy & psychology whom also influenced Hegel and others.

"Education should aim at destroying free will so that after pupils are thus schooled they will be incapablethroughout the rest of their lives of thinking or acting otherwise than as their school masters would have wished ... The social psychologist of the future will have a number of classes of school children on whom they will try different methods of producing an unshakable conviction that snow is black. Various results will soon be arrived at: first, that influences of the home are 'obstructive' and verses set to music and repeatedly intoned are very effective ... It is for the future scientist to make these maxims precise and discover exactly how much it costs per head to make children believe that snow is black. When the technique has been perfected, every government that has been in charge of education for more than one generation will be able to control its subjects securely without the need of armies or policemen."

[Bertrand Russell quoting Johann Gottlieb Fichte, the head of philosophy & psychology – Prussian University in Berlin, 1810]

This system like all other subversive tactics or methods being used in forwarding any given specific and hidden agenda. There outer exterior is always presented colorful and positive while concealing there true face and intentions or agenda. And the brainless sheep masses will believe and follow, as they are blindly led to the slaughter.

I have maintained time and time again that this body dose NOT! operate in the best interest of America, and the American people. The Common Core system, is no more then a specially tailored and designed state Curriculum, designed so to subvertly indoctrinate or Desensitize students.

The objective is not so much but dose include the altering, changing or miss presenting of information. But rather it is a system specially designed so to alter the viewpoint of students in how they perceive, interpret or understand any given political, social or religious issue or situation.

The exact model of this state sponsored system under different or variant names has and still is used in countries such as Iran, China, Cuba, Venezuela, North Korea and the former Soviet Union. The root and core of this system was in fact first developed in 1810 by Johann Gottlieb Fichte, who was the head of philosophy & psychology whom also influenced Hegel and others.

In one Common core study text book, president Obama is referred to as a nice guy or a good guy.I would like to point out that the problem isn't that Obama was mentioned..But the fact that a political figure has been presented as a " good guy " or " A nice guy " in it self is a state initiative or objective and that is where the problem lies, And why?.

For the fact that a child should be taught free will or the ability to think openly and for him or her self. The fact that a political figure has been presented to the young and impressionable mind of children, Is a clear violation of that fact. Because it is instilling a pre-determined view point or mined set in to the mined of children, which as time progresses and this process is continued over a period of time.

The pupil becomes convinced or perceives the state as good unconditionally. A view point which he or she will not have obtained through investigation or research or the result of independent thought process but rather it will stem from a pre-designed and embedded perception initiated by the state.

The Common Core, system is in effect divided in several stages or levels with each stage preparing the student/students for the next. Like other subversive methods this tactic also requires a long period of time to be complete and is a lengthy process.

Chapter

Seven

STATEMENTS & QUOTATIONS BY AUTHOR

" Government becomes a problem when it becomes infested or saturated with members of the business/ Corporate sector. It is only in such a scenario which government is no longer limited. Government must only comprise of men and women from the common ordinary citizenry, men and women whom are first foremost statesmen and not businessmen, the two sectors must not at any time merge. "

-Darius Radmanesh

" In my opinion its is not a question as to which group with in society has control over capital, now rather it be the state or the private sector..for me its about no single body having absolute control over the capital..that is the main point here. Because ultimately at any time, any single group holds the power of total ownership over Capital, the inevitable outcome will always be corruption, and that the value of production and currency must be only established based on the principle of supply and demand. And not be determined by the Banks, Wall-Street or the state, it should be those whom actually are the producers to determine the value of there produce or the worth of there labor. The system which Hamilton created (Corporate Capitalism) is with out question a system designed to benefit the wealthy elite (The Minority) both private and state, whereby excluding the rest of the populace in society, the common man (The majority). "

-Darius Radmanesh

" I must make one point abundantly clear. I am a stout and devout supporter of a free laissez-faire economic system, which is void of any influence or control by the state...To be exact I advocate the economical system which was created by the great French economist Destutt de Tracyand, which was in turn also strongly supported by Thomas Jefferson...However, that being said I would also like to make one point very clear..A point which I have already addressed in my theory " Proletariatism ", Which is that I do not in any way harbor any animosity towards Capitalists/Corporatists or any other group with in the Commercial sector. My main and only reservation with regards to the mentioned groups.

Is there involvement or meddling in matters of state. If Capitalists/Corporatists, can stay out of politics and simply focus their time and energy on what they know best which is the areas of finance and industry. Then more power to them, only as I have also pointed out the merging of Capitalism with politics and ultimately it replacing the political state with a economical system in its stead or establishing state Capitalism (Socialism) or State Corporatism, is ultimately the inevitable objective of Capitalism. So regrettably I do not think or believe that Capitalists will ever be able to pull away from politics. After all, thier sole objective is to generate monetary or capital profit..More the better...Thus what better guarantor can a Corporate Capitalist possibly have, then being involved in politics and therefore being able to curve legislation which will ultimately help to increase his or her profits or gains?? "

-Darius Radmanesh

" When I use the term merge when referring to the over stepping of the commercial sector in to the affairs of state. I am in effect referring to the halls of Government being filed with members of the business or Commercial sector, or worst yet, that the political state is in effect replaced with a purely economical one. I would like to elaborate my point here. The kind of people we need in our government are those whom are statesmen and women, first for most. Individuals whom have never at any point in time either in the past or the present have been involved with or have held any shares, investments or capital interests with in the business or commercial sector. Their sole purpose for entering politics must be with out exception to serve there country period. They must be statesmen or politicians nothing else, now the reason a individual whom prior to becoming involved with politics was in the business or commercial sector, should not become involved in politics.

Is simply because he or she will always be a businessman or woman first and then a politician, and why?. Simply because such individuals have already tasted and have already experienced the luxurious and comfortable life which a successful and lucrative business life can offer. Therefore such people are tainted with what I call the capital Bug, meaning that no matter what endeavour they undertake no matter what there initial intentions may be even if they are sincere at the start. Ultimately in the end they will succumb to the itch and fever for acquiring or accumulating wealth, plain and simple there is no way around it. I suppose the proper or correct term for such a state of mind is in fact...GREED. "

-Darius Radmanesh

" yes I am a strong believer in the free market system however, I do NOT! believe in nor do I advocate Capitalism. Because ultimately Socialism, and Capitalism, are in fact both ethically and principally the very same. "

-Darius Radmanesh

" In my opinion its not a question as to which group controls the capital, now rather it be the state or the private sector for me its about no single body having absolute control over the capital with in society that is the main point here. Because ultimately at any time any single group holds the power of total ownership over Capital. The inevitable outcome will always be corruption, and that the value of production and currency must be only established based on the principle of supply and demand and not be determined by the Banks, Wall-Street or the state. It should be those whom actually are the producers to determine the value of thier produce or the worth of thier labor. The system which Hamilton created (Capitalism) is with out question a system designed to benefit the wealthy elite (The Minority) both private and state, whereby excluding the rest of the populace in society (The majority). "

-*Darius Radmanesh*

" In America today, the state is no longer a political entity serving the civil and social interests of the people. But rather instead it has been transformed in to a purely economical system focused exclusively on the pursuit of generating capital profit, In short It has become simply nothing more then just a Corporatist/Business body. "

-*Darius Radmanesh*

"Corporate greed was the cause for my mothers suffering and untimely death and countless others like her. So how could I possibly hold it with any other sentiment other then total and complete disdain and contempt, this most vial of of all evils?"

-*Darius Radmanesh*

" He (Hamilton) in effect put in to place a system which ultimately has enslaved a entire nation, whereby the average ordinary common citizen, has become the slave of the wealthy/Corporate elite . Whom perceive the common man as no more then a commodity very much like live stock or cattle, with only one purpose. So to produce for their elitist masters capital profit. So in effect the tragedy of slavery in America not only has it NOT been truly eradicated. But rather with regards to the ever increasing power and hold of the Corporate elite over not only American society but rather also over all other peoples of the world. It is very clear and evident to me that in effect the tragedy of slavery is still very much alive and real today. So we can conclude that this is still a case of slavery, only this time it doesn't concern a specific race or group of people with in society as it was the case before the American civil war. But rather this time all of mankind is in threat. "

-*Darius Radmanesh*

The difference between Proletariatism

& Marx's Dictatorship Of The Proletariat

Dictatorship of the Proletariat basically refers to a certain life style which is enforced upon all members of society period with no exception...It dose not however imply the superiority of one class or group of citizens over another, but rather it enforces the concept of a universal or single economical/social system on all citizens.

Under Marxism, everyone in society are to live in accordance to one standard. Meaning that no one is permitted to own private property or to accumulate private wealth, however my theory this is not the case. under my theory the owning of private property or personal wealth is not prohibited.

The only issue which is enforced is which group of citizens are able to run for and hold public office, which are the members of the Common citizenry. All members of the minority elite the Corporatists and members of the Commercial sector are not.

This however dose not mean that they are not permitted to maintain there wealth or there commercial interests etc. On the contrary as I have maintained time and time again. So long of course that they do so with in their respective boundaries and limits, also I think that it is important to point out that in addition-

that both their social and economical rights with in society are not discarded or violated or infringed upon, unlike under Marxism. Only their political rights are restricted.

This is of course do to the fact that any time the world of finance or industry is permitted to gain access in to the realm of state. The inevitable out come is always political corruption, a free prosperous industry and economy is good for society as a whole.

My only reservations is that the commercial sector remains out of the countries political affairs. That's it, plain and simple In this aspect my theory is very unique and novel.

Also it is not in any way a economically based theory, such as capitalist or Marxist/Socialist ones its core principle as I have stated is purely political and socially based, its sole objective is to put in to retrospect which group of citizens should have the ultimate say and control over the affairs of state.

Rather then legislating and dictating policies and laws made by the minority to be forced upon the the majority which only serves the interests of a minor section of society. It makes it possible whereby the fate and lives of the majority is in effect placed back in to their own control and hands.

By transferring the power and control of the state over to the common/ordinary citizens with in society (The majority) taken from the power and influence of the elitist minority whom push forward legislation and other laws so to forward their own business and financial interests at the expense of infringing upon, the freedoms, rights the interests of the majority which are the common ordinary citizens.

-Darius Radmanesh

" We Americans, must stop assessing the goodness , success or even failure of a society purely based on its economical achievements or standards. We need to start looking beyond economical and monetary aspects with in society and start jugging a system purely on the bases of its moral and ethical standards. As I have always maintained, " A free people will always be prosperous, but a prosperous people may not always be free ".

-Darius Radmanesh

" National sovereignty is in fact the most fundamental and most important pillar of political state. Simply because Sovereignty is with out question vital in establishing political authority and political accountability. Which clearly proves that people shape their own destiny collectively. Therefor, we can conclude that any institution or body which forwards or advocates the abolishing of sovereignty (National sovereignty) and internationalism or Globalism in fact are NOT! political entities bust rather they are economical in short (Corporatism). And why?, for the simple fact that as I have explained, you cannot have a political state with out national sovereignty, I mean if we look at lets say even empires.

The concept of an empire even though involves the control and ownership of vast territories/countries etc. By one nation or state In such a scenario we are still dealing with one sovereign nation at the helm, because empires are ultimately political institutions. However if we now draw our attention to the economical institution of Corporatism. We will find that in the view of the Commercial/Corporate institutions, national boundaries, borders or even sovereignty's are not recognised, and that all territories, lands and peoples are free game and are not off limits when Capital/Business interests are concerned. "

-Darius Radmanesh

" What kind of world do we live in today I ask?, where ones worth and value is judged and determined not by the principles and virtues of integrity, honesty, loyalty, morality and honor. But rather by jinglings of the coins and wads of notes one carries in his or her pocket?. These are the only recognisable virtues and Worth's of man, in this empty, dark and gilded shell which we so shamefully perceive to be the only true symbols of society!. "

-Darius Radmanesh

" I am a strong believer in the school of life.....Yes acquiring a academic education is very important. However the education which one receives at school, University etc. is highly dependent on and limited by the material and information which is made available to the students. Information mined you which can, and are in many cases easily altered and tailored so to fit with, or forward a specific state or global objective and agenda. Therefore, I believe that it is absolutely imperative that one also opens his or her mind to the many social and political events taking place around them. Because an academically acquired education covers only 30-40% of ones education the remaining 60-70% is in fact gained from life. "

-Darius Radmanesh

" Party politics is not what America needs so to address the many crises which she is facing today, rather it be the two main parties or to replace these with another...To replace one party or political entity with another is simply continuing or repeating the statuesque. By doing so we are in fact merely addressing the symptom but not curring the ailment or cause of the problem. What America needs is the adaptation of Proletariatism in to very core of her political apparatus."

-Darius Radmanesh

" The issue here is not rather a person is wealthy or not, but rather buy what means has the individual gained or acquired his or her wealth, this is the question. A If a person such as a framer, small business owner or restaurant or even small food store owner becomes wealthy through hard work and applying initiative and ingenuity, then this is what I call healthy or positive wealth. This is for the simple fact that such endeavours will not only bring prosperity and advancement to the individuals in in question, but in addition it also has a positive impact upon not only his or her local community, but rather also the over all well being of his or her country as a whole. This is for the simple fact that in such scenarios, individuals contribute to the economy of their communities by not only utilizing both local labor and material resources and thus providing work and jobs for the men and women with in their community and society in general.

They also provide a positive and necessary service which have a positive impact upon there local communities. However with regards to Corporations this is not the case. With regards to this body, their only and sole interest and drive in life is the hording and accumulating of wealth..period. There are no qualms or reservations as to how this objective is achieved, so long as it is achieved. Any and all measures or steps forwarding this single objective are acceptable with no restrictions or moral restraints on how they are carried out. So long as the end result is profitable, hence the old saying...(The end justifies the means). "

-Darius Radmanesh

THE DIFFERENCE BETWEEN THE TERM HUMAN LABOR

& MY NEWLY COINED TERM CAPITAL-LABOR

The two definitions of Human capital and Capital Labor, do seem to be the very same, however in fact they are not. The first " Human Capital " is a business or Corporate term and is defined in the Oxford English Dictionary as follows:

" The skills, knowledge, and experience possessed by an individual or population, viewed in terms of their value or cost to an organization or country. "

However my new definition refers to the locally based positive Capital only, which is generated exclusively by the individual on a local bases such as with in the jurisdiction of a city, county or state.

Capital Labor, not only refers to capital produced by the individual by means of manual labor, but it also refers to capital which is then reinvested or put back in to the local community,

In the form of creating jobs or work for members of the local community by utilizing the local labor force and natural and other forms of recourse's and materials. As apposed to Human capital , which defies the overall view point or assessment held by Corporations with regards to the value or economical impacts of manual labor on a much broader spectrum which is both on a national and international levels.

-Darius Radmanesh

" My new term Capital-Labor is not Social capital, I would rather refer to it as the core building block or force with in the foundation of the free market system and a free society, which is essentially the individual at the local or community level. as apposed to being a commodity very much like live stock or cattle whereby its only worth and value is measured only by its marketability or market value. A view point which is held by the internationalist/globalist Corporate elite. "

-Darius Radmanesh

" The United states constitution...Is not a reflection upon the intelligence and wisdom of our founding fathers. But rather it is a testament of a generation, whom had first hand experienced the horror of life under tyranny and servitude. "

-Darius Radmanesh

" When the majority of citizens with in a society are in control of there own destiny, we have freedom, liberty and prosperity. However when the future of a people is not in there own hands but rather is determined by a fraction of society (The wealthy Corporate elitist minority) we have enslavement, tyranny and suppression. "

-Darius Radmanesh

"So long as the Commercial sector or the world of business and finance remains with in its own respective boundaries, It can bring prosperity, productivity and a strong economy to society. However, once it spills over in to as I have pointed out the world of politics or even religion. The inevitable outcome is almost always corruption of these institutions."

-Darius Radmanesh

A word of advise to all my fellow countrymen and women In the coming elections, before you cast your voter and support a candidate, first make sure that he or she dose NOT! have any ties, connections or dealings with any section or part of the Commercial sector. Be sure that he or she is from a humble background and is from the ordinary common citizen body. No mater what do NOT! allow your selves to be deceived and manipulated by the fancy and sugar coated rhetoric of the corporatist. These men and women are experts in the art of bartering, selling, and negotiating business deals, and make no mistake folks, for them running for office is just that...IT IS A BUSINESS DEAL...Plain and simple.

They are out for number 1...They do NOT! care nor are they interested in the sufferings, troubles and difficulties of the ordinary citizen. They have only one objective here, to enter office so to push forward thier own financial and monetary gains and bussiness interests. So do NOT! be deceived, what and how they say or speak may sound pretty and may seem sincere and true. However that is simply board room and corporate talk. They follow the motto " Say and do every thing and any thing so to seal the deal, That's it. The entire process is no more then a show, a farce and a scham. When you find out that a candidate has any ties or dealings with any area of the Commercial sector, You must turn and walk...NO!...Run.

-Darius Radmanesh

"When the world of finance is merged with the world of politics we have corruption, And the inevetible consequence of political corruption is always state suppression and totalitarianism."

-Darius Radmanesh

Simply put statesmen and women belong in government, businessmen and women belong in the private sector. The only active roll the state should play or have when dealing with the Commercial sector, is two points:

1- First two enforce the laws which protect contracts etc.

2- To maintain low taxation and very minimum to no interference in the countries economical affairs.

Thats it, these are the only active roll the state should have in any dealings with the private or Commercial sector... period.

-Darius Radmanesh

" A free economy is not the foundation or pillar of a free society...But rather it is the consequence of a free society governed by a free people, in other words. A free economy is not the cause of a society being free, but rather it is the byproduct or result of a free society. "

-Darius Radmanesh

" We the generation of Americans, today are not cowards, but rather we are a byproduct of the subversively desensitised or indoctrinated last two generations. "

-Darius Radmanesh

" Some such as Montesquieu and John Locke , have argued that man by nature is inherently good or others such as Hanfeizi and Thomas Hobbes, have argued that man is by nature bad, others such as Aristotle, have even maintain that he poses both. I however must disagree with both counts, In my view man in his most basic and purest stage which is the time of his or her birth, is void of both evil or good, but rather his or her soul is like that of a blank canvas clean and pure. Now rather upon reaching adulthood man harbors with in his heart the spirit of good or evil, is entirely dependent upon the environment or surroundings of which he or she has been exposed or subjected to during his or her developing years. "

-Darius Radmanesh

" Political parties in the United states have become the bridges with which the commercial sector uses so to cross over and gain a footing in to the state. Thus they have been reduced to being no more then lobbyists for the Corporate elite. And party politics is nothing more the Corporate or Office politics being carried out on a grand scale forwarding their agenda and objectives. "

-Darius Radmanesh

" Corporate greed was the cause for my mother Linda Kay Mckim's suffering and untimely death, and countless others like her. So how could I possibly hold it with any other sentiment other then total and complete disdain and contempt, this most vial of of all evils?"

-Darius Radmanesh

" Marxism/Socialism/Communism are not now not ever have they at any time been ideologies or systems created so to forward the cause of the common man. But rather they are ideologies set in to place so to forward the objective or agenda of the globalist corporate elite. After all, after the success of the Bolshevik revolution in Russia (The October Revolution) which group of the citizenry wier massacred in their millions by the Bolsheviks?...Answer..The common citizens..The peasants. "

-Darius Radmanesh

" I find it to be an outrage and true tragedy whereby in our society today, the terms Common and working man have become synonymous with leftist ideologies of Socialism, Marxism or Communism. When in fact not one of the mentioned degenerate institutions of the left have even in the most remote since contributed to addressing the many plights, struggles and hardships which the Common man has been forced to face and endure...

If any thing, such a stigma has in fact increased the difficulties of the common ordinary citizen. Simply for the reason that no one with in a free society will ever admit publicly of being a member of the common citizenry or the working class for the mentioned reason. For fear of being tagged as a Commie or Socialist....

And right here lies the dilemma, simply because If any given issue or problem is not permitted or allowed to be discussed either by the state or simply because the issue at hand happens to be socially not acceptable, how then can the issue be properly addressed and a effective solution to the problem be found?. The example for this is that the first step towards recovery for an alcoholic is first to admit (Publicly so) that he or she has a problem,

Then and only then is such an individual ready to move on to recovery. This is the very same situation with regards to the social even political stigma of one calling him or her self a member of the Common citizenry or the working class. To me the dark cloud which this perception or stigma has cast upon society is in fact perhaps the single greatest triumph for the Corporate elite, whom have with one swift move been able to silence the voice of the common man. "

-Darius Radmanesh

" Political parties in the United states have become the bridges with which the Commercial sector uses so to cross over and gain a footing in to the state. Thus they have been reduced to being no more then lobbyists for the Corporate elite. And party politics is nothing more the Corporate or Office politics on a grand scale forwarding their Corporatist agenda and objectives. "

-Darius Radmanesh

Here is some food for thought America, there are so many reasons as I have pointed out many times over as to why the wealthy Coporate elite should not be permitted entry in to the halls of government, however here is one very important point I would like to share with you as well.

Every time you see our Congress, which mined you is filled with men and women of the wealthy elite, is not doing its job or is selling out there constituents, you the American people by allowing our rights, freedoms and liberties to be trampled upon or so easily give in when the slightest pressure is applied upon them,

Just remember one very important fact. The richer and wealthier an individual is and the more worldly positions he or she may have, consequently the more he or she has to loose. The point I am trying to make here is this....

If the halls of Congress is filled with men and women from the Corporate sector, whom posses a great deal of wealth and business interests or investments in the Commercial sector, and are faced with a scenario whereby they have a choice to either fight for and uphold the rights of the American, people and to uphold the laws set forth in the United states Constitution.

However in result of this possibly face putting at risk there business and financial interests and investments, how do you think they will act?. Just ask your self this question the next time you are about to vote for such a candidate.

-Darius Radmanesh

" I must profess that I am at times speechless, dumbfounded and even stupefied at the level of hypocrisy and total unawareness even ignorance and delusional stance of many with in the so-called well educated and learned members of American society today with regards to so many fundamental issues facing not only America..But rather also the rest of the world. "

-Darius Radmanesh

Being a member of the working class or of the common citizenry is not a fashion statement or even a state of mind, But rather it is a way of life.

-Darius Radmanesh

" For a wealthy individual whom lives a life of luxury and comfort void of any hardships or struggle, to present him or her self as a member of the working class or of the common citizenry, simply by altering his or her exterior appearance. By wearing simple and at times tattered clothing. Is like saying that an impoverished person is wealthy simply because he or she wears a suit or makeup. After all, being a member of the common or working class is not a fashion statement or even state of mind, but rather it is a way of life. "

-Darius Radmanesh

America, the solution for the many crises and challenges which our country is facing today both economical and political, is not pined upon party politics, individual candidates or simply adhering to the same old political tactics and approaches etc. Because at the end of the day these are all either of very little or no consequence or have been corrupted by various elements such as either foreign intrigue or by the wealthy/corporate elitists.

Whom are bent upon turning not only America, but rather the entire world in to one massive plantation and for you and I like slaves to cultivate it for the sole purpose of generating capital and material profits and gains for our elitist masters. No America...

If you wish to reclaim our country and to reinstate the sacred principles of Freedom and ,liberty and the laws and values which had been set forth and intended for America, by our founding fathers back in to the fabric of our nation, then there is only but one solution. That is for the people to demand that Proletariatism, is implemented in to the political apparatus of our country.

To achieve this, no new constitutional amendment is needed to be add nor is a Constitutional Convention required to be held. This is because Proletariotism, is simply a political/ideological tool which can easily be added to our countries existing current system, without having to alerter or change a single law or principle. Proletariatism, will in fact act as a safety valve or safety mechanism which will safeguard and protect the very laws and principles which had been laid down by our founders. Once Proletariatism has been added,

Its political and economical impact in America, will be dramatic and almost instantaneous. Whereby both the control over the government and the economy will immediately be removed from the influence of the Corporate elitists, and instead will be returned to and placed under the direct supervision and control of the people.

-Darius Radmanesh

" Party politics is not what America needs so to address the many crises which she is facing today, rather it be the two main parties or to replace these with another. To replace one party or political entity with another is simply continuing or repeating the statuesque, by doing so we are in fact merely addressing the symptom but not curring the ailment or cause of the problem. What America needs is the adaptation of Proletariatism, in to very core of her political apparatus."

-Darius Radmanesh

Its not about the Democratic or Republican parties etc. Because ultimately both or even possibly all parties in the United states has been at some level infiltrated by the Corporate elite. Also its not about individual candidates either, most Americans, believe that ..." hey If one official doesn't do their job right then we will just vote him or her out and elect someone else "...

With out realising it we are simply continuing the same cycle and statuesque over and over and over again with out ever at any time changing or altering the policy, objective and direction of the state...No matter whom we elect regardless of which party the candidates are representing. In the end its always business as usual and nothing changes. You know why America??, because its not down to or dependent upon individual candidates, because ultimatly even if a candidate is truly sincere and honest and dedicated to the cause of upholding our countries sacred document the United states Constitution and the over all well being and interests of the American, people

In the end its not about what a elected official wants or not. But rather its about what policies and objectives his or her party wish to push forward, You see what I am saying here America?.

Lets say for example in a presidential election we vote for and elect a certain man or woman , which we believe to be best man or woman for the job? etc. Ok, Lets say he or she gets in to office. You know who's policies he or she will be pushing though and enforcing?, not yours or mine that's for sure. No sir,

He or she will do exactly what they are told by thier party's committee...PERIOD!...And you want to know why?. Because which ever party he or she is representing, if the candidate chooses to do things his or her way and totally discard the will of thier party...Guess what?. Coming next term the Republican party will withdraw their support and endorsement and will not nominate and back his candidacy, and not to mention any and all legislation which he or she may try and push though in both Congress and the Senate will be automatically ignored and discarded

Plain and simple. You see America, right here lies the core dilemma and cause of our countries many issues and problems. Because we the people for far to long have been living under the false perception or should I say (Delusional perception) that all we need to do is to elect the right candidate etc. or back the right party....WRONG!.

Now as for the parties them selves well, they regardless of which one you support or back, in turn are as I have explained before. They have been reduced to being nothing more then Lobbyists for the Corporate elite, forwarding their globalist objectives and agendas...period.

 After all, is this not the reason why the Corporate elite have for so long monopolised the political system in America?. Whereby making sure that elections are so expensive, so complex and restricted, whereby it has become almost impossible for a ordinary average citizen in America, to be able and take part? and thus be able to enter the highest offices of government, and consequently hinder their (the Corporatists) agendas and objectives?.

-Darius Radmanesh

" In America today, the state is no longer a political entity serving the civil and social interests of the people. But rather instead it has been transformed in to a purely economical system focused exclusively on the pursuit of generating capital profit, In short It has become simply nothing more then just a Corporatist/Business body. "

-Darius Radmanesh

With regards to Unions in the United states under the Proletariatism system. Under Proletariatism, no body or entity rather it be Unions or political groups or organizations which in any way perform as a special interest or lobby group, Which forward any political interests or objectives for the Corporatists will be permitted to operate. Only those Unions will be permitted, are those whom their sole purpose and objective is in fact to uphold and forward the rights and interests of the workers/employees etc. which they are to be representing

Secondly, ordinary members of society the common man, are not Corporatists and therefore are not attempting at curving any legislation so to forward their own personal interests. So no these restrictions do not apply to them, It only applies to Corporatists elite body's, Banks, Mega Industrialists etc. and not the average citizen.

Also I would like to add that even though in most cases with regards to Unions, members will take part in various Union operations marches, rallies etc. being organized by their Unions which do in fact at times forward the interests of various disreputable political figures and objectives etc.

Fact of the matter is that the sole responsibility of such measures and actions are not to be placed on the backs of the average citizens which join these Unions. But rather it is the leadership of the Unions in question whom should be held exclusively accountable for deceiving, miss informing and miss representing Union members as to the true nature, cause and objective of such measures.

-Darius Radmanesh

THE NATURAL CITIZENSHIP CLAUSE

IN THE U.S CONSTITUTION

What many Americans, do not understand with regards to the Natural Citizenship clause in the U.S Constitution is that, our founding fathers were addressing a matter which was by far much more important then only the physical aspects of a citizens place of birth. Rather they in fact were also addressing the moral and emotional implications or aspects as well.

Basically the question we Americans should be asking, is not just rather or not a Candidates parents at the time of his or her birth were in fact natural citizens, or even if the Candidate was in fact born on U.S soil or not. Of course this is very important, only we must also ask: In which country was the Candidate raised and why?? This is very important because the location or environment of a child's upbringing, especially at a very young age.

will ultimately be responsible in forming the mind set, and the child's view on life and society when he or she reaches adulthood. In other words.. who or what a child will be as an adult, will depend immensely on, which culture or country he or she was raised and educated. We can conclude that even though a child may very well be born on U.S soil, depending on how young he or she was when they were taken and raised in a foreign country, and exposed to a foreign culture.. when that child has grown to adulthood..

he or she may very well have very little or no recollection of their country of birth. So consequently, they would feel very little attachment or sense of kinship with that country or its citizens. Not only is the location of birth very important, but also even more vital and crucial.. is the country and culture in which the child was raised and exposed, and how it will reflect on what they were most influenced by in their developmental years.

MULTIRACIALISM (YES)

MULTICULTURALISM (NO)

The problem is not Multi racialism or racial integration but rather Multi Culturalism, because the race of a people signifies only the physical differences between one group of people and another, such as there skin color or the various attributes of there facial features etc.

however, Culture is the very foundation and soul of any given society to merge or integrate two races is like fusing or Grafting the leafs or stems of two plants or two trees together. In nearly all such cases there is no problem and the plant or tree will continue to grow and flourish, however, were you to try and perform that same operation with the roots....that plant or tree WILL! surely die.

The culture of any given society is like the roots of a plant, it is the very life source, foundation and identity of any given society, you tamper with that or try and merge it with other cultures. it will lead to the lose of national identity and will consequently bring about the collapse and demise of that society.

-Darius Radmanesh

LIFE EXPERIENCE AND TYRANNY

when trying to understand or learn about the horrors of tyranny and oppression. Life experience is perhaps the greatest of all acquired education, surpassing any knowledge attained with in the confined four walls of a class room.

-Darius Radmanesh

ORGANIZING A CONSERVATIVE MOVEMENT

When organizing a Conservative, rally, march or protest, one must always refrain from labeling it or attaching any identifiable banners or slogans, which can be used by the opposition as a means to tag or label the movement as either right wing extremist or fringe etc. After all an enemy that cannot be labeled or identified is very difficult to react to and ultimately difficult to defeat, hence in the words of Saul Alinsky where he stated that:

Pick the target, freeze it, personalize it, polarize it

In other words

Identify it...label it....then Destroy it

**-*Darius Radmanesh*

THE DECEPTION OF STATE ORGANIZED MOVEMENTS

When the state is about to implement certain changes to the Constitution or laws of a Republic, which may generate an unfavorable reaction from its citizens, and so therefor may result in wide spread out cry and possibly revolt towards the state, it is imperative that the state in turn takes the necessary precautions and measures so to both secure and protect its position. It can do so by creating a safety valve whereby this powerful and potentially dangerous energy can be contained and channeled towards an objective beneficial to the state.

so that it cannot in any way hinder or challenge the state and its objective, while in the same since allow a means for the people to express and vent there angers and frustrations under a controlled environment, while giving the people the delusion that they and not the state are in control of the situation...so now the question is this, what form of environment would be most sufficient, suitable and most effective in bringing about such a task?

the best way for a state to contain, control or channel the progress or direction of a revolt, uprising or even a revolution, is that it (The state) IS THE ONE WHO INITIATES AND ORGANIZES IT! (with out the people having any knowledge of this of course).

this way it can monitor and control the direction of any given movement or uprising while at the same time giving the people a life line whereby they are able to channel there frustrations and concerns, while at the same time they pose no threat to the position of the state, or the states objective.

-Darius Radmanesh

POLITICAL CANDIDATES PROMISING TO

SAFEGUARD OUR FREEDOMS

" When I hear a candidate running for office say that he or she will be fighting to defend my freedoms and liberties. I ask, have you ever experienced life with out these principles? and if not, then how could you possibly comprehend life with out them? consequently how could you possibly know what it entails to safeguard mine? "

-Darius Radmanesh

THE TRAGEDY OF SOCIALISM

The tragedy of Socialism, is that at the beginning its deception over the masses is complete....however ....the realization of its deception after the fact is almost always instantaneous...and once Socialism has secured its roots with in the very fabric of any society.....it will require the suffering and sacrifices of many generations after, before it can ever be uprooted.

WHY I AM DEVOTED TO AMERICA?

My unshakable and uncompromising devotion to America, and the sacred cause of freedom and Liberty, can be best summarized for the following reason:

Freedom suppressed again, and again regained, bites with keener fangs than freedom never endangered.

-Cicero

I have personally experienced the chains of servitude, oppression and tyranny. It is for this reason, that when I was finally able to regain my freedom, I loved and cherished it even more so then those whom have always lived unchallenged in its light and radiance.

-Darius Radmanesh

A NATION DECEIVED

" A nation who's citizens have never experienced tyranny, and in consequence are not able to understand and recognise the face of a tyrant, is doomed to be deceived and ultimately enslaved by tyrants. "

-Darius Radmanesh

RULES & LAWS WITH IN SOCIETIES

" In societies governed by law, we have Justice and freedom, In societies governed by rules, we have injustice and suppression. "

-Darius Radmanesh

ECONOMICAL PROSPERITY, BUT!
VOID OF FREEDOM

A life with economical prosperity but void of freedom, is like slavery, where the people are bound in chains of Gold and Silver. "

-Darius Radmanesh

UNDERSTANDING TYRANNY

The tragedy of tyranny is that it cannot be taught or explained, but rather, it must be experienced first hand before it can ever be truly understood.

-Darius Radmanesh

DISCRIMINATION ON THE BASES OF SKIN COLOR

Any man whom discriminates against his fellow man simply on the bases of the color of his skin, rest assured holds a very special place in the bosom of Lucifer.

-Darius Radmanesh

STATE DECEPTIONISM

State Deceptionism, refers to a political maneuver or safety measure which is covertly orchestrated and executed by the state. Which consists of a movement or uprising initiated by the state, at times of wide spread revolt and civil unrest. Such fabricated movements by the state, are contrived covertly and the origin's of such movements are not disclosed to, and are kept hidden from the the people. citizens in such a scenario are given the allusion that they (the people) are the instigators and not the state.

The purpose of such movements are to contain what may potentially become a dangerous force against its (the states) position and authority, but rather also be able to channel it in a direction which will consequently not only be pacified and made harmless. But may also be able to harness this force and use it to its own advantage.

RULES & LAWS WITH IN SOCIETY

" Rules are always created by the state (The minority) to be enforced upon, and obeyed by the people, (The majority). Laws on the other hand are made by the people (The majority) and are to be adhered to and to be abided by all. "

-Darius Radmanesh

LAWS MEAN FREEDOM, RULES MEAN TYRANNY

" When the elected leader of a free society, replaces laws
with rules, he or she is no longer is a leader of a free people,
but rather is a usurper and tyrant. "

-Darius Radmanesh

TYRANNY OF MONEY

" Money is like a Dictatorship, it binds and casts you in chains, and like a
Dictatorship, in order to live and survive you must bow your head and
submit to its rule, when in your heart you detest and despise it. "

-Darius Radmanesh

EVOLUTIONISM VERSES CREATIONISM

Creation is not a Science, it is spiritual and is based on faith and the
concept or theory of evolution is not a Science either hence its name "
Evolution Theory ". So basically it is a principle or idea which is based
entirely upon a theory and is backed by no conclusive or solid scientific
or tangible evidence?

so therefore, the whole concept of evolution theory is basically just like the concept of
creation and is based entirely upon a belief or having faith in a idea?. so, why then are
we to believe that the idea of creation is wrong and incorrect?

while the idea of evolution is right and logical?, When they are both entirely faith
based?. So we can conclude that the theory of Evolution and the idea of creation are
in fact both a spiritual idea or concept and not a scientific one!.

-Darius Radmanesh

" During my years in captivity in Iran, for me the allure of the American
dream, was not the prospect of economical opportunity. But rather It
was the intoxicating hunger and desire for freedom.

-Darius Radmanesh

THE DIFFERENCE BETWEEN

RULES AND LAWS

The defining difference between Laws and rules is basically which group or body of citizens are putting these edicts in to place, the majority or the minority?. The Majority being the common ordinary citizens with in society or the Minority which is the state.

when laws are put in to effect in Republics which are governed in accordance with a set number of guidelines, regulations, checks and balances put in so to safeguard the rights of the people (such as in the United states) or in Democracies, whereby though there is no Constitution per-say

any and all new legislation's are however put forth before the people (The majority) to be voted on. So in both cases either by adhering to guidelines of a Constitution in Republics or obtaining the consent or vote of approval by the people as is done in Democracies.

In both cases the freedoms and rights of the common ordinary citizen (majority) is protected and safeguarded against the infringement of there rights by the state, whereby all legislation which is passed in this matter becomes law. However when any new legislation is put forth or forced upon the people by the state

SHOULD A LEADER BE LOVED OR FEARED?

This question has baffled rulers and leaders for centuries, however in most cases we find that the later option is preferred, this is simply for the fact that to obtain total and complete love of the people is near to almost impossible, and even if attainable it is just as difficult to maintain therefore, the policy of rule by imposing fear is adapted.

I personally however object to both of these options, for the following reasons. Yes as pointed out to gain the complete and total love of the people, is extremely difficult and yes even if achieved, to sustain it for any long period of time is nearly impossible, and why?. For the simple reason that the love which a people will develop or have for there ruler/leader is a love is based not on any solid footing like the love one would feel towards a loved one or a blood relative.

Therefore, it is a very unstable and fickle sense or feeling, which stems directly from emotion, and emotion is almost completely influenced not by any personal sense of obligation like to ones family member or any since of devotion like one feels for his or her spouse.

But rather it is influenced by turn of events and any given circumstance at the time therefore, it can change from one moment to another, and it is for this reason this option is not practical or dependable. As for the second option, to govern or rule by imposing fear. This option is also in my opinion not practical and in fact is more dangerous and its effects more damaging then the first option.

This is because when a ruler/leader chooses to govern his or her people through fear, this generates a great deal of secret inner resentment and anger towards there leader, a resentment which will lay quite and dormant until an opportune moment, then the people will at that time reek vengeance against him,

therefore to govern using this option is highly unstable and dangerous. It is for this reason I also do not advocate the second option either. I for one choose a third option, which is respect, whereby a ruler or leader governs by establishing a sense of respect from the people towards both him self and his administration.

Because respect is a sentiment which dose not stem from the irrationality of emotions nor is it a sense which provokes anger or resentment, it is a sense which simply derives from reason and observation.

Meaning that so long as a leader, treats the people with respect and courtesy, and dose not in any way infringe upon both there personal or civil liberties or rights, or does not in any way violate there honor or self respect and is always just. the people in return will also act accordingly with respect to there leader, this is because as I have pointed out, the response or reaction of the people stems from reason and not based on irrational emotion hens the old saying " seeing is believing ". Therefore so long as a leader, maintains this approach towards the people, they in turn will continue thier support of his or her government.

" Banks are perhaps the most vial of all Corporatist entities ."

-Darius Radmanesh

" We must throw out all Corporate elitists from the halls of government and place in their stead, men and women from the common ordinary citizenry, whose sole objective and interests are not the lining of their political and financial pockets, and the interests of only a fraction of society. But rather the glorious cause of our beloved America and the combined interests of the great American people. "

-Darius Radmanesh

National sovereignty is in fact the most fundamental and most important pillar of political state. Simply because Sovereignty is with out question vital in establishing political authority and political accountability. Which clearly proves that people shape their own destiny collectively.

Therefor, we can conclude that any institution or body which forwards or advocates the abolishing of sovereignty (National sovereignty) and internationalism or Globalism in fact are NOT! political entities bust rather they are economical in short (Corporatism) and why?, for the simple fact that as I have explained, you cannot have a political state with out national sovereignty.

I mean if we look at lets say even empires the concept of an empire even though involves the control and ownership of vast territories/countries etc. By one nation or state. In such a scenario we are still dealing with one sovereign nation at the helm, because empires are ultimately political institutions.

However if we now draw our attention to the economical institution of Corporatism. We will find that in the view of the Commercial/Corporate institutions, national boundaries, borders or even sovereignty's are not recognised, and that all territories, lands and peoples are free game and are not off limits when Capital/Business interests are concerned.

-Darius Radmanesh

SUBVERSIVE DESENSITIZATION

Subversive Desensitization, Refers to a process which covertly alters or changes a persons mind set, consequently transforming his or her perception of reality with regards to either Social, political or religious matters. Whereby rendering a person incapable of understanding or viewing a situation presented before them in a clear and rational manner.

Subversive Desensitization, is the ability for radical extremists either religious or political, in being able to deceive or manipulate the populace in submitting to there extremist ideology or doctrine. With out seeing or understanding the very serious and potentially dangerous implications of there actions.
[*New term coined by Darius Radmanesh on Mar 2, 2014*]

TWO FORMS OF REVOLUTIONS

There are two forms of revolutions, the first is Civil revolution. Civil revolution is basically when the citizens or the people of any given country rise up against thier government this is done for two reasons:

1- in apposition to specific laws or legeslations being enforced by the state. In this case the people may not necessarily be revolting so to over throw thier government but rather only demand that these specific laws are either reformed or done a way with all together. Secondly, another reason for a civil revolution would be of course for the purpose of ousting of a countries reigning government in favour of establishing another.

2- the second form of revolution is what I refer to as " state iniktiated revolution ". In this case its not the people whom rise or revolt against the state, but rather it is the government which turns against the people. In the case of State revolutions, it involves a transition where the state transforms from one entity to another. For example, when a Socialist government transforms to a Democratic one or visa verse, however I think that its important to point out that when a states transitional process Intel's a Socialist government transforming in to a Democratic one...

this transition is usually very public and citizens are made fully aware of what is taking place. However, in the case of a free state which may be either a Democracy or a Republic, is being transformed in to a Socialist or Communist state. In this situation the transition is done very covertly and is kept very quite and away from the public view. A process which in most cases may require several years for such a transition to be completed, this of course is for the obvious reasons. Almost unanimously the citizens of a Socialist state will support a transition to Democracy, however when the government of a free state wishes to transform in to a Socialist one....

the people of the country in question will vigorously oppose it. Therefore, any government of any free state who wishes to implement or to transform their system of government to a Socialist or Communist one, must in order to achieve this, over a course of many years very gradually and subversively implement certain elements of the new doctrine in to the various cultural and social areas and fabric of society...

whereby ultimately undermining the very foundations of that specific society, which will then ultimately bring about the total collapse of that countries political, social and cultural foundations .

-Darius Radmanesh

CENSORSHIP, HOW DOSE IT WORK?

When the state of any free society where freedom of the press, speech and expression is the law wishes to implement censorship (State sponsored Censorship) it must do so through a specific process which is referred to as " Subversive Measures ". This process is comprised of two levels or stages. These are as follows:

1- Mild or covert censorship
This is the initial stage where the state very quietly and in some cases even stealthily implements censorship to specific material and information, rather it be with regards to information shared through the media, or material used in cinematic movies, TV. Shows etc.

Or information and material used in the educational institutions. Of course Censorship isn't just about withholding information but rather in some cases it is also about altering and even changing the core message or character of a message regarding any specific issue or subject.

These highly subversive tactics are used primarily at the early stages of the Censorship implementation process. Simply because the citizens of a free society whom have become accustomed to being free with expressing there thoughts and views with out any fear of reprisal or state regulated restrictions.

If at the beginning become aware of the states intentions. This would lead to wide spread unrest and anger amongst the populace and would ultimately result in a revolt against the state by its citizens. So therefore if the state wishes to implement such a process it must do so very quietly and slowly.

The most important aspect of this process is not so much the citizens forced adherence to censorship, but rather implementing this process in such a manner whereby the populace will subconsciously after a period of time abide by this rule them selves with out the need of any physical encouragement forth coming from the state.

Meaning that the exposure of the people to this process is don so in such a low amount and over such a long period of time that censorship becomes almost second nature and is perceived as simply the norm and is accepted as the reality of every day life. Another consequence of this process is that not only will the citizens in question abide by or adhere to state censorship willingly, but also even those whom openly profess to appose censorship and are ardent supporters of free speech and freedom of the press etc..

Will ultimately them selves with out knowing it exercise censorship against those materials or information which they do not agree with or perceive as not in accordance with what they believe to be correct or acceptable.

They do so with out understanding that if one supports the principles of free speech and freedom of expression, then one must adhere to these principles at all times and not only when it suits them or when they choose to do so. its like saying that one is a devout Christian and whole heartily believes in the Bible, but picks and chooses what parts of the Bible he or she are willing to adhere to?. This level or stage of Subversive Censorship can take anywhere from 5-10 years for it to be complete.

2- Overt or aggressive Censorship.
At this level all material and information is openly and officially Censored, whereby before any new material or information is either broad casted or publicised it must first be presented to the state and only upon received the states approval will they be permitted to be publicised.. This includes all material used in movies, on Television and in the media. Also all information and material taught to students at all levels in all educational intuitions across the country.

In addition, as shown in the first stage, nearly all citizens with in the society in question have come to accept censorship as the norm. However there still will be those with in society whom will refuse to allow them selves to be manipulated or indoctrinated by the state. So, it is required by the state to enforce its censorship rule by means of force. Censorship at this level is for a indefinite period of time.

TERMS & THEORIES COINED MY THE AUTHOR

-Discriminatism

Discriminatism is a act of violence or aggression stemming from discrimination towards a specific group or citizen body with in society. Committed either Overtly or Covertly. Discriminatism can be based on race, gender, faith, age, social, class, or political standing .

Discriminatism a violent act committed (Overtly or Covertly) against ethnic minorities.

Discriminatism a violent act committed (Overtly or Covertly) against the elderly in Nursing HOMES.

Discriminatism a violent act committed (Overtly or Covertly) against one group by another, simply based on there religious beliefs

[*by Darius Radmanesh January 03, 2014*]

-Capitalutionism

Refers to the three inevitable Evolutional stages of Capitalism. This process is categorised in to three consecutive levels or steps.

1- Economic Capitalism: All focus and activity is exclusively involved with matters of Finance and Industry.

2- Crony or Corrupt Capitalism: This refers to a process whereby Capitalism spills over in to politics and via various special interest or lobby groups it is able to influence government legislation and policies etc....

3- State Capitalism or Socialism: This refers to when Capitalism ultimately replaces the conventional national government or political state and essentially becomes the state or system of government.
Capitalutionism, is the progressional evolvement of Capitalism in the United states for the past two or three centuries. Whereby, Capitalism initially at its conception was a purely Economical system focusing exclusively on matters of finance and Industry. However over time it has evolved and has been transformed in to a major element with in American, politics.

[by Darius Radmanesh January 01, 2014]

-proletariatism

It is a non Socialist or Communist political system. It is the concept of a principled statesman driven system of government which is overseen exclusively by elected members of the common working class citizenry. Proletariatism, is very unique in comparison with traditional political systems in that its core principle is neither party politics driven, nor economically driven like in the Capitalist/Socialist systems. Proletariatism, is a system of government which aims to foster and FORWARD the joint activism of the working class majority allowing them the ability to become more involved maters of state. Proletariatism, is a system to be adapted in to any free government state, which can be either a Democracy or a Republic.

[by Darius Radmanesh December 28, 2013]

-LABOR CAPITAL
Labor Capital, Refers to capital or wealth which has been acquired through the application of manual labor or hard work which includes but is not limited to, Building, Construction work, Farming or Mining etc.

a- John's Labor Capital, has been very lucrative this year.

b- Mike's Labor Capital, from farming was verylucrative this year.

[by Darius Radmanesh July 03, 2014]

-Subversive Desensitization

Subversive Desensitization, Refers to a process which covertly alters or changes a persons mind set, consequently transforming his or her perception of reality with regards to either Social, political or religious matters. Whereby rendering a person incapable of understanding or viewing a situation presented before them in a CLEAR and rational manner.

Subversive Desensitization, is the ability for radical extremists either religious or political, in being able to deceive or manipulate the populace in submitting to there extremist ideology or doctrine. With out a person seeing or understanding its serious and potentially dangerous implications or consequences.

[*by Darius Radmanesh March 06, 2014*]

" The state in America, today and the Corporate/Business sector are ultimately the very same body. There are no longer any defining lines with which you can separate them . "

-Darius Radmanesh

" Some argue that if we do not select or elect our leaders from the wealthy Corporatist/Business citizenry, then the only other option or alternative would be to elect those whom are either Community organisers (Leftist/Marxist individuals or groups), men or women of the cloth even or lawyers?. To such statements my answer is that why must we either submit and bow before the Corporatist elite, or to Marxists, religious leaders or attorneys?.

Why not instead we place our faith and hope in the hands of the very people whom have been from the beginning the builders and pioneers of our great country. They whom have fought in and have died in every war America, has taken part in right from her conception, the common citizenry.

Men and women such as the hard working blue blooded American farmer, fire fighters, police men, lumber jacks, carpenters, builder, factory workers, school teachers, College professors and soldiers etc. The common citizenry (The majority) These are the true builders and life blood of America, therefore it is these whom also should be at the helm of our government, and also to have a decisive and final say as to how our country is governed, and not the so-called elitist/ wealthy Corporatists (The minority). "

-Darius Radmanesh

Thats how the left operates eventually every avenue or venue which they have initially utilised in order to forward their objectives, Once their usefulness has been exhausted they then terminate it. The same way they use democracies,they use the power of the ballot box to gain a footing in to government. Then once that objective has been achieved they then turn and eliminate the very same system which had assisted them in their objective.

As I have said this is common Marxism plain and simple, In fact they dont stop there. Once Marxism/Socialism has been completely established as the sole power with in any state, one of the first steps to be taken by the newly established leftist state is to immediately exterminate or execute nearly all high profiled or prominent members with in the many Marxist/Socialist groups or parties which had assisted in their rise to power.

This is classic Marxist behavior or ammo, they have repeated this process in every country which they have been able to gain control of. So yes, Once the "Employment Non-Discrimination Act," has exhausted in purpose then they will in turn eliminate it simply because they don't want its powers to be used against them selves by their enemies or opponents. Like I said, Classic Marxism.

-Darius Radmanesh

Only members from this group of citizens are permitted to run for public office to thus become active members of there countries politics. Whereby citizens who belong to the wealthy, elitist groups, or upper class, the minority Capitalists, consisting of Industrialists, Bankers, large manufacturers, Corporations, etc. are prohibited from ever running for or holding public office at any level.

Many will argue that our law enforcement in America, has collapsed. The reason for this tragedy is in fact very simple. That is because there are no longer any laws to enforce, but rather what we have now are rules.

And so therefore our old legal enforcement system which had in fact been established so to enforce the laws of our nations founding document, and other laws which in that same effect were put in to place so to safeguarded the civil and social rights, also the freedoms and liberties of the people, is no longer viable or relevant.

For the simple fact that the intent or purpose behind the new rules, is so to bring about an objective which is ultimately in direct contrast to, and to undermine the very purpose and reason behind the creation of those laws.

-Darius Radmanesh

" A leader must live by example, this also includes his immediate family, when the nation is facing a serious financial or other form of crises, therefore the citizens of his or her country are facing difficult times and are expected to make certain sacrifices . It is a leaders duty to follow suite and do the same ...a leader must always place the interests of the nation before his or her own, and must always live by example. "

-Darius radmanesh

" I envision a day when the common man shall rise and will break free from the chains of servitude with which greed has enslaved him, and he will stand as the undisputed heir and master of the earth, as it was intended in the beginning. "

-Darius Radmanesh

NOT THE END

BUT THE BEGGINING